Compassion and Truth

Compassion and Truth

Why Good Intentions Don't Equal Good Results

Daniel J. McLaughlin

Battle Creek Books

To my wonderful friends in Africa,
thanks for encouragement and inspiration

To Ruth, Matt, Ben, Kara, and Tim,
with love and respect for your unfailing support

Contents

Part 2

A Common Understanding

Part 3

Discussion of Policy Prescriptions

Foreword

"You shall know the truth," said Jesus (John 8:32), "and the truth shall set you free."

The immediate context in which Jesus spoke those familiar words prompts many Bible scholars to assert that their meaning is strictly spiritual. In the previous passage, it's clear that He was addressing believers, especially those who converted that very day: "If you hold to my teaching, you are really my disciples." The words of John 8:32 advise believers that Jesus is not only the conveyor of truth but the essence of truth itself. Believing in Him liberates one from the lies and snares of a sinful world and promises an after-life where truth will reign supreme.

But in the larger context of how we should arrange our lives and relationships in this physical world, truth liberates in other ways too. Christians should not find this surprising. The God who created humanity would be inconsistent and inexplicable if He intended his creations to be free spiritually but slaves in every other way.

At least that's how I see it as an economist and a Christian, and that's why I commend this book by Daniel J. McLaughlin—not just to Christians, but to anyone who appreciates the truth.

Economics is the study of purposeful human action in a world of limited resources and unlimited wants. Properly understood, it explains an immense volume of human behavior and activity. The starting point for it all is not some collective abstraction such as "nation" or "society" or even the more localized concept of "community." It all begins with the only thinking, acting, decision-making entities on the planet—specific, identifiable individuals without whom none of those abstractions would make sense or even exist. We are not a world of pre-programmed, identical robots. Each of us is unique, which means that to be fully human, we must be free to exercise our uniqueness through our personal choices.

Governed by law that protects each individual's inherent right to *be himself*, a free economy is both human and humane. An *unfree* economy means that some people (those with political power) can suppress or even prohibit the peaceful, voluntary, and mutually-beneficial interactions of consenting adults. A little bit of that may be tolerable even though it's harmful, but a lot of it is called slavery, and that makes possible what a pretty good wordsmith once coined as "man's inhumanity to man."

Informed by his Christian principles, Dan unravels the beauty of a free economy in this book. It truly is a miraculous thing, which is what we should expect. Each unique, individual human that God created acts to improve his or her material well-being. That leads us to specialize (the division of labor) and then trade with each other, leaving both sides to voluntary transactions better off than if we ignored or fought each other. Moreover, no top-down, mandate-issuing dictator could possibly know a fraction of the supply and demand information that emerges naturally and spontaneously in the form of prices.

Everything of value has a cost that somebody must pay. Nations become wealthy not by printing money or spending it, but through the capital accumulation *of* individuals and the subsequent creation of goods and services *by* individuals. Higher standards of living, if they are not to come at someone's expense, can only come about through greater production and trade, sound money, and the ethical values that keep us honest, responsible, and future-focused.

When people have little or no economic understanding, they embrace the "quick fix" and support impractical "pie-in-the-sky" solutions to problems. They may think that whatever the government gives must really be "free." They don't know the difference between the budget deficit and the national debt. They might even think that trade is a bad thing, that if we shut the borders to the flow of goods our living standards would rise. They will not only be unable to see through economic and political snake oil, they won't be able to identify its harmful consequences either. In the absence of sound economics, a lot of what starts out sounding "compassionate" ends up doing real harm to real and innocent people.

As Dan explains and illustrates, a free economy rests upon indispensable institutions and conditions. Private property is one and justice (to each man his due) is another. Between the Golden Rule and the Ten Commandments alone, property and justice would seem to enjoy a solid Biblical foundation. But there's much more to a free economy, much more to what Christianity says about how and why humans function best when they're blessed with one. Right here in one very accessible volume is a whole lot of what a compassionate person needs to know so his compassion really can do good, and only good.

When you're finished with *Compassion and Truth*, you will have learned a great deal about the science of Economics. You'll understand its connection to Christian ethical values. You'll see how this knowledge can lead you toward the right policy prescriptions for improving human lives and away from the seductive but destructive, dead-end proposals that enslave and impoverish. You will have the truth, and if enough of us stand by it and practice it, it will make us free.

Lawrence W. Reed
President
Foundation for Economic Education—www.fee.org
Atlanta, GA
October 2015

Preface

Why Read This Book?

This book is a response to Christian teachings on economic matters, but the ideas discussed are not explicitly Christian. It uses the Bible as a reference because interpretations of its meaning are the justification for economic teachings of the churches. The same understanding is applicable to any sacred text used to support economic policies. All interpretations are not truth, but are, rather, beliefs about the truth.

Truth is independent of beliefs. If something is true, it doesn't matter what the proponent believes or what, if any, religious affiliation he or she might adhere to. All truth is a part of God's ordered world. Things happen a certain way in nature and society, without regard to good intentions, personal preferences or political ideologies. If you are reading this page, I assume that you possess some level of compassion and concern for others and that you want to do what is right. You want to make this world a better place. So do I.

What if I told you that too many people are dying in plane crashes and that I wanted to help, so, out of my compassion, I developed an antigravity machine to prevent devastating crashes? You're not buying it? How about if I could show you reams of reports with complex mathematical formulas and present a plausible case based on extensive experimental work I recently completed? I imagine that nearly everyone would tell me to go back and do the experiments again, because they violate everything that is known to be true in modern physics. The experiments obviously contain errors and the theory is wrong, even if I really, sincerely want to help people. Relying on those experiments may actually cause more death.

No matter how many good, positive, helpful uses I can propose for the new development, how good the intentions are, or how plausible the case I make for it, planes would still crash and people would still die. As the old saying goes, you can't fool Mother Nature. Natural laws still hold, no matter how strenuously you argue against them. Along the same lines, I can't make water flow uphill or build a perpetual-motion machine or turn rocks into bread.

From another perspective, what if I told you that prices are too high to allow people on fixed incomes to put food on the table, and gave price controls, a legal maximum that sellers could charge for their products, as the solution? That would help the elderly and the poor live better lives. What if I told you that families are living in poverty because they aren't earning enough at their jobs, and, therefore, we should also impose minimum wages at a level high enough to sustain them? Poor families would then be able to make ends meet.

These too can be supported by plausible arguments, complex statistical models, and thick reports from smart people. As we shall see, however, economic laws hold just as true as physical laws do, even in the face of emotional, heart-rending circumstances or scientific-sounding reports. Maximum price controls below the market price cause shortages, and minimum price controls above the market cause gluts just as surely as stepping off a high ledge causes broken bones or death. The same laws applied thousands of years ago, as the rulers of ancient Egypt, Sumeria, and Babylon, along with their victims, discovered.[1] Economic laws are cold and

---

[1] Robert Schuettinger and Eamonn Butler, *Forty Centuries of Wage and Price Controls,* (Washington, D.C.: The Heritage Foundation, 1979), 9–11.

heartless, as are the laws of physics. It is up to us to know our limitations so we don't get hurt or inadvertently hurt others.

Many people feel a strong and growing disconnect between the requirements of the Christian gospel and the policies of modern church and society, which are influenced by plenty of drama and emotional stories. There is a growing discomfort with laws that fly in the face of the Commandments and a concern for the continuing discord that is being sown in our society and the world at large, all in the name of helping people. The discomfort is a good thing. It is a starting point for inquiry.

If you feel some level of discomfort, maybe this book is for you. Maybe it will answer some questions or give you a new perspective. Maybe it will confirm what you already know. Maybe it will turn the light bulbs on in your head and spark an interest in learning more. There is a whole lot more to learn. God's laws have always been there to teach those who make the effort to understand. There is an underlying law, a reality that existed even before the commandments were handed down to Moses and upon which the commandments themselves are built. Even before large-scale societies emerged, the world worked according to fundamental principles. It is up to us to discover them and live in harmony with them as best we can.

The Apostle Paul described spiritually immature people, those without knowledge of the truth, as infants. They are "subject to every wind of teaching and the cunning and craftiness of men in their deceitful scheming" (Eph 4:14–15)[2] because they have not learned to look at the world through the eyes of truth. That world is confusing. The Christian gospel doesn't seem to fit with the contemporary understanding of economic reality.

---

[2] All Bible references are taken from the New International Version, Copyright 1985 by the Zondervan Corporation, except where noted. All biblical references will be given after the quotation in parentheses, with the name of the book, followed by chapter, a colon, and then verse or verses.

To many people, contemporary economics appears to be a jumble of incoherent theories and political motivations, merely a justification for legal plunder by the elite in business and government. In a certain sense they are correct. The economics profession has morphed into a high-stakes game that seems to stack the deck in favor of the powerful. It is understandable that many Christians oppose business and markets in general and harbor a disdain for all of economics. In another very real sense, however, they are not correct. Their vision of economics has been grossly distorted and is not an adequate explanation of reality.

The basic premise of this book is that reality reflects God's truth and the order that He[3] created. This work is not an attempt to justify economic theories, with the gospel as a standard, but rather to demonstrate that, in truth, there is absolutely no conflict between Christian theology and sound economic principles. It is the recognition that there is an underlying harmony that is open for discovery.

True economic laws simply describe the reality with which human beings deal in their everyday lives. They don't change with the times, fashions, or religious and political affiliations. Sound economics doesn't have to be justified or harmonized with the gospel, any more than chemistry, physics, or biology does. It is the way God's world works. It only has to be defined and understood. Though the Bible was not intended to be an economic treatise, it describes real people in everyday situations. It illustrates particular circumstances and people's reactions to them. Thus, the stories demonstrate the universality of economic laws over time and place. This book includes many biblical references for that purpose, regardless of whether anyone accepts the significance of those scenes for contemporary religion.

---

[3] The masculine "He" is used for God in keeping with the usage in the biblical text.

Many Christians are sincere in their belief that their job is to bring about the kingdom of heaven here on earth. They intend to use every tool they can to achieve what they think is right. The problem with much of that thinking is that many of those tools hurt the very people that they are designed to help. They ignore reality, God's order, and the unchangeable and unyielding laws governing this universe and the human race. More to the point, abusing the economic laws with political interventions in the economy will lead to inevitable, predictable outcomes that hurt people and damage economic relationships. No matter how good the intentions, the result will be bad for the victims of such policy.

This writing starts with the assumption that God's word is truth, and that if we live our lives in harmony with that truth, we will be more likely to live happy, productive, Godly lives and contribute to the well being of all people. That doesn't mean that everyone's life will always be rosy and problems will be nonexistent. It only means that using the right roadmap will point us in the right direction. Using the wrong roadmap will get us lost. We are lost because we are using the wrong map.

Economic thinking is merely truth in human action. It has little to do with mathematics and everything to do with choices. It is consistent with God's Commandments and everything that Jesus said. In essence, economic truths are a reflection of God's eternal truth. That is not to say that everything that goes under the name of economics is based on truth. Many people have an understanding of economic phenomena that relies on half truths, incoherent political ideologies, or fairy-tale wishes. Others are convinced that economics has to do only with money and requires complex calculus and an advanced university degree to comprehend.

My intention in writing this book is to present a more accessible understanding of economic concepts, to show how they describe the underlying reality behind biblical and historical events, and to give you a better grasp of the real, inevitable, and often negative consequences of economic policies. I hope that it will give you more confidence in dealing with issues of the day and help you more easily to recognize economic fallacies that are so common in society.

It is unfortunate for the victims of bad policy that many modern church officials inform their theology with faulty economic thinking rather than informing sound economic thinking with good theology. The modern church has a substantial impact on politics, and politics wields a very heavy hand in economic outcomes. A serious stumbling block is that people don't have the economic tools to help them understand the issues, or, significantly worse, the analytical tools that they have been given are not based on economic reality.

As you go through this book, judge what you read by what you already know about reality and how it all fits together. Some ideas may be hard to accept at first, because they seem to fly in the face of conventional wisdom. If that is so, take the time to argue the case in your own mind and see if it reconciles with the real world.

Everything that Jesus said or did implicitly recognized the laws of nature. While we may not understand the miracles of the Bible, what we now call the laws of physics were assumed to be in effect in Jesus' time, just as we assume them to be effective today, whether we understand physics or not. If you step off a high place, you will fall. A heavy object takes more force to move than a lighter object. The angle at which you throw something will affect the distance it travels. We count on those truths to order our daily activities.

The same principle holds true for economic laws. As we shall see in the coming pages, economics is more than money and trade. Those laws affect everything that human beings do. They affected the actions and decisions of even the most primitive man or woman. They have always operated the same way throughout human history, whether or not we like them or understand them. They are principles that cannot be broken. We can only break ourselves, our lives, our people, and our world upon them. They are proverbial lighthouses, which can help us stay away from the rocks when we follow their guidance. Ignoring the principles only invites disaster.

My hope is that this writing will help to keep us away from the rocks, to recognize the wonder of God's world and the order that He provides for free people, and to understand how economic laws help us to live in harmony with one another and His amazing creation.

Daniel J. McLaughlin

The Ten Commandments (Ex 20:2–17)

I   I am the Lord your God… You shall have no other gods before me.

II   You shall not make for yourself an idol…

III   You shall not misuse the name of the Lord our God…

IV   Remember the Sabbath day by keeping it holy.

V   Honor your father and mother…

VI   You shall not murder.

VI I   You shall not commit adultery.

VIII   You shall not steal.

IX   You shall not give false testimony…

X   You shall not covet your neighbor's house. You shall not covet your neighbor's wife, or his manservant or maidservant, his ox or donkey, or anything that belongs to your neighbor.

The Law of Love (Mt 22:37-40)

Jesus replied: "'Love the Lord your God with all your heart and with all your soul and with all your mind.' This is the first and greatest commandment. And the second is like it: 'Love your neighbor as yourself.' All the law and the Prophets hang on these two commandments."

The Golden Rule (Mt 7:12)

So in everything, do unto others what you would have them do to you, for this sums up the Law and the Prophets.

Introduction

I do not feel obliged to believe that the same God who has endowed us with sense, reason, and intellect has intended us to forgo their use. —Galileo Galilei

God created a wonderful world. He created it with an amazing order. Things happen for a reason, and there is a cause-and-effect relationship for everything that occurs in the world and in our human lives. Though we may not know specific causes in every instance, we are able to discern certain laws of nature. They help us to understand how the physical world works and to use those laws of nature to build a better life, to provide more food, higher-quality shelter, improved transportation, and so on.

Human society is also subject to a certain amazing order. While human relations and events are not strictly predictable in the same sense that the trajectory of a flying object is predictable, they are subject to some simple laws that have not changed over the course of human history. If that was not so, chaos would continually reign, planning would be futile, and society would not exist. Rather than chaos, however, there is a fairly high level of predictability in our daily lives. The future is truly unknowable, but there is normally a certain regularity we can count on around which to build our lives. This book was written with Christians in mind, but you don't have to be a Christian to understand it and accept everything it says about economics. Like the physical laws, economic laws don't depend on creed. The main theme is that Jesus' words and actions represent universal truths that are timeless and reflect the natural laws that have always been and will always be true.

An important presumption in this work is that Jesus proclaimed the gospel of freedom. He said: "If you hold to my teaching, you are really my disciples. Then you will know the truth, and the truth shall set you free." (Jn 8:31–32) The apostle Paul said: "You, my brothers, were called to be free. But do not use your freedom to indulge the sinful nature; rather, serve one another in love. The entire law is summed up in a single command: 'Love your neighbor as yourself.'" (Gal 5:13–14) Freedom is a frequent theme woven through the gospel. Whenever Jesus called anyone or admonished anyone, that person always was given a choice and was never forced to comply. He recognized that many would not choose his way.

He said "Enter through the narrow gate . . . . But small is the gate and narrow the road that leads to life, and only a few find it." (Mt 1:13–14) Yet, without the freedom of choice, nobody can choose to follow or not to follow. Without freedom to choose, virtue is dead.

The only political system that is consistent with the gospel of Jesus is freedom. Any system based on aggression, coercion, and/or theft defies the commandments of God and is entirely inconsistent with the gospel of Jesus. He displayed his contempt for the governing class of his age numerous times. The Pharisees, Sadducees, and temple officials were all a part of the ruling elite. Like most politicians today, they piled burdens on the people and made detailed rules to restrict their lives. They followed the letter of the law, but still cheated and were dishonest. They exalted themselves at the expense of the people.

As in Jesus' time, the truth today is often denied, and those who speak the truth are frequently ridiculed. The impetus for this book came from the realization that much of what passes for truth today, especially in the realm of economics, is based on half truths or outright falsehoods. The misunderstandings and half truths justify political policies that cause much of the conflict and dislocation in society. Unfortunately, a large proportion of the official policies of religious, charitable, and government organizations nowadays is founded on economic fallacy and not on universal truth.

Much of what passes for wisdom in this age is a resurrection of the errors of old—of fallacies that have been repeatedly demolished. It was also that way in biblical times. The book of Proverbs repeatedly makes a point of foolish people rejecting wisdom and knowledge.

Bad policy often falls under the guise of helping the poor, the oppressed, and the downtrodden. Jesus reminded his disciples on a regular basis of the importance of true charity. But he also gave us the parable of the two sons. The father commanded his sons to go into the field. The first son refused, but later decided to go and do as his father had asked. The other son told his father that he would obey, but did not go into the field to work. Jesus asked "Which son did the will of the father?" (Mt 21:18–31) Obviously the first son did, even though he originally said no.

That parable is a very powerful lesson. It doesn't matter what you say you are going to do. It matters what gets done. Many policies of churches and secular governments are feel-good statements about caring for the poor and the oppressed. They reveal, however, a complete misunderstanding of the source of long-term poverty and blindness to overt systematic oppression. Actually helping the poor and the oppressed in the long run only comes from actions that give the result of less rather than more and continued poverty and oppression.

There is also often a blatant disregard for the commandments and the teachings of Jesus. Stealing and aggressive violence, under the cloak of government programs, substitute for charity.[4] Class

---

[4] In order to redistribute resources to one person, they must necessarily be taken involuntarily from someone else. Taking someone's resources against his or her will is theft. People can only delegate to organizations and governments those things which they, as individuals have a right to do. People have no right to steal from someone, and thus, they cannot delegate

conflict is encouraged, and covetousness is exalted and lifted up as a way of life. The gospel of secular socialism puts on a moral façade and poses as the gospel of Christ.

When the commandments and the natural laws, physical and economic, are disregarded, the results will be less beneficial than expected, or as is often the case, downright disastrous. This can be seen in development economics of the last four or five decades, a favorite subject of adulation for churches and politicians. While the stated goal is less poverty, the methods employed have merely entrenched oppressive governments and squandered the resources of people who believed they were making a difference.

The result is what Peter Bauer, one of the very few earlier development economists who advocated economic freedom, called the three Ms of development economics—monuments, machine guns, and Mercedes; monuments to the dictator, machine guns to keep him in power, and Mercedes Benzes for him and his cohorts. This is the case of the second son. Because economic truths and freedom were ignored, the result was that the work of the father was not done. To the extent that they are ignored in the future, the result can only be more of the same: extended misery among the world's poorest and most oppressed people.

The first part of the book will present the economic laws in a way you may not have heard before, and describe how they fit with God's nature and with the words and actions of Jesus. The second part will discuss definitions of some familiar terms for common

---

that right to government. When the government takes property from citizens, it is backed up by threats of violence or actual violence. That is why governments must be held on a very short leash. It is a dangerous servant and a fearsome master, in the words of George Washington. Government power is the source of tyranny. The understanding throughout this work is that the legitimate role for government is limited to the protection of the rights of individuals. This idea is developed further in Section 2, Good Government, on page 110.

understanding. The third part will be a detailed look at various policies promoted by people and organizations that, while they may seem plausible on the surface, are in conflict with economic truth, the gospel of Jesus, and the will of the Father. The final chapters summarize the types of things that Christians can do as part of God's free people in addressing the many problems plaguing our country and the world.

Part 1

Economics Is About Real People

1. You Are an Economist

Buy the truth and do not sell it; get wisdom, discipline and understanding (Prv 23:23)

Whether you know it or not, you are an economist. You make the decisions that you do because you expect certain results. From your life experiences, you know that things generally happen a certain way. You adjust your behavior to get the results that you want. That is a fundamental understanding. Things don't always turn out the way you wish they would, but at the time you make your decision, you believe that your choice will give the result you desire, or at least the best result given the available options.

While you may not have formally studied the laws of economics, you have some level of understanding of the way society works, some recognition of the idea of cause and effect, and some basis for making rational decisions. That is, in essence, all that economics is. It is an understanding of the laws that govern human action, which hold true for individuals as well as for the whole of society. As with the physical sciences, either we work within the framework of reality or we suffer the consequences of defying immutable natural law.

There are many definitions of economics. The textbook definitions typically have to do with the use of scarce resources for the production and distribution of goods and services throughout a society. While that does capture part of it, the concentration on the physical commodities and measurable events narrows the focus too much and leaves out some important areas for discussion. In the author's opinion, it misses the essence of economics. It is a view of economics in a narrow sense.

For the purposes of this study, we will use an expanded definition of economics, which is more inclusive and general, one that leads to a better grasp of economic reality. The core concept, the foundation for economic understanding, is that all people use specific means to achieve their specific desired ends or goals. That may seem trivial and straightforward, but it is actually a quite profound understanding, the importance of which regularly eludes many highly trained mathematical economists.

The Bible is filled with descriptions of people using means to attain ends. It has to be. Without human choices, means, and ends, there would not be much to report. People do things because of the results that they expect. They have goals in mind, as well as ways to achieve them.

There are some means and ends that we may think of as good, some that we think are bad, and the choice over which goals to pursue is subjective, subject to our values. Values refer to one's moral judgment system. Our values determine what we think of as good and bad.

The width of a table can be measured objectively by using a ruler, but the width of a table cannot be good or bad. The measurement is not subject to discussion on the basis of values and morals. It is only a way to describe reality. The width of the table can only make it suitable or unsuitable for the intended purpose. The same can be said of economic laws. They are descriptions of reality and are not subject to discussion of moral rightness or wrongness. They can only be true descriptions of reality or not true descriptions.

The purposes themselves, the goals, and the means chosen to achieve them, however, do depend on our background, our preferences, and our assumptions about the future. They can be considered good or bad, based on our value system. The Bible guides us as Christians in our general thinking on morals or values and what goals we should seek.

For each goal, there are various ways to attempt to achieve it. Once the goal is set and the method chosen, the effectiveness of that method in reaching that goal is less a function of values. It is more objective, based on measurable reality, much like the width of the table. Will the method chosen actually get you where you want to go? That is subject to cause/effect relationships, to the immutable laws of nature, and the laws of economics and human action. In this way, economics can be helpful in understanding the way things work. It can help to look beyond the presumed goodness or badness of an objective and determine whether an action will really lead to the desired result.

The atomic bomb is a particular combination of elements and processes that yields predictable results. Was the dropping of A-bombs on Japanese cities good or was it bad? Some say that it was good because it cut World War II short and possibly saved more lives and prevented more destruction than occurred in those blasts. Others say that it was definitely bad because so many innocent civilians were killed and maimed. The goodness and badness is a human judgment, which depends on each person's assumptions about reality. It is entirely independent of the nuclear reaction.

That is a crucial aspect of understanding economics. Many times an action is chosen because we believe that the end result will be what we consider good. An objective look at the means to attain the desired ends, however, may reveal that, no matter how good the intentions are, the end result will likely be bad. If someone is very sick, you may sincerely try to help by giving that person a poisonous substance, believing it is a cure. In spite of good intentions, your chosen method of helping will likely end in death.

The core of this work is that God's word is truth, and if we live our lives in harmony with that truth, we will have the best chances to be happy and productive and to contribute to the well-being of mankind. Conflict arises when we don't live our lives in harmony with truth and the reality of natural law.

God's Ten Commandments and the Christian gospel help us to decide what our goals should be. They are the basis for our moral foundation and judgments. As Christians, we look to the Bible to inform our choices of goals. Choosing a career or marriage partner, deciding to buy a house or throw a party or help the poor are examples of the millions of decisions we make about what we want to accomplish and where we want to end up. In each case, there is some uneasiness that drives us to seek a specific goal. If we are hungry, we set a goal to eat. There are, quite literally, thousands of ways that we can satisfy that goal, and each carries a different expected cost and benefit.

There are certain laws that we have to follow without fail, the natural laws that can never be broken. Conservation of matter, action/reaction, momentum, and gravity are such laws. We face them every day and, most often, successfully navigate through them. They are in complete harmony with God's will. While we each may not know all of the scientific explanations, we know, in general, how the world works.

A football quarterback may not know a single thing about the theories of physics. He does, however, know the laws of physics and adjusts to them every time he throws the ball. If he adjusts correctly, he hits his target. If not, he misses and presumably learns from his failure.

There are laws of human action, or economics, which are just as valid and just as harmonious with God's word as the law of gravity. The first step in understanding economics is to realize that we are all economists. We deal with economic reality every day, and so we are better economists than many highly trained academics, who, in their professional capacity, may deal only with theoretical models and numbers and then try to impute their artificial expectations onto real people. We act economically all of our lives, even when it doesn't fit nicely into the theoretical economist's convenient mathematical systems. The people in Jesus' time and all throughout history were equally effective economists.

We need to state formally and explicitly some concepts that we all know from our own experience so that they will help us in understanding and clarifying the phenomena that occur in our lives. It is much the same as defining the basic laws of physical sciences so that we can get better results from the things we do. The problem with economic phenomena is that the results are often far removed from the cause, or included in so much tumultuous activity that they are unrecognizable as such. It is similar to the turbulent ocean surf pounding the rocks. You can't make any sense of wave motion in that situation, but the simple laws that dictate the motion of a single wave also dictate the results of a confusing mess of interacting waves.

Simple economic laws govern what happens in human affairs in the same sort of way, even when causes and effects are masked by a seemingly endless chaos of the markets. It is only chaos because we cannot comprehend the millions of separate inputs occurring at any time in a complex system. The resulting interactions are complex but the laws governing them are simple.

In the following pages we will see how economic principles harmonize with the message of the gospel. We will deepen our understanding of those concepts, relate them to reality, and, in the last section of the book, analyze official policy positions based on our understanding.

In mainstream economics, the subject is divided into micro and macro economics. Microeconomics is the study of economic laws and how real people interact in a society. Macroeconomics is the study of the overall economy using aggregated statistics and mathematical models. It ignores the reality of individual choice. Macroeconomic analysis suffers from significant theoretical and practical limitations that preclude its legitimate use as a tool for rational decision making on a national or regional scale. The critical issue with macroeconomics, as presently practiced, is that it gives politicians ideological cover and a pretense for manipulating markets and people. It is a justification for interference in voluntary transactions in a market economy. It is the source of a great deal of incoherence and the politicization of the practice of economics. Most of it does not add to a true understanding of economic reality and the development of prosperous societies and is, therefore, believed by the author to be irrelevant to this examination. This is certainly a controversial point of view, and Appendix 2 has a more in-depth discussion of macroeconomics.

Inherent in all of Jesus' discussions was the idea of choice, the freedom to make decisions, even if that meant that some people would choose unwisely and make mistakes. Jesus gave the rich young man the choice of selling what he had and following him, or not. The man went away, because he thought the cost was too high. Jesus didn't force him. (Mk 10:17–23) He allowed the Samaritan woman at the well the choice of turning away from sin. (Jn 4:7–26) He allowed his disciples to make the choice to follow him. That is critical to the understanding of Jesus and morality.

People can only be good and act morally under free will. Jesus had harsh words for the governing class of his day, the Pharisees, the Sadducees, teachers of the law, and temple officials. He called them blind guides, vipers, liars, hypocrites, cheaters, and murderers. (Mt 23:13–36) They bound up the people with rules and regulations and didn't lift a finger to help. Doing this didn't teach the people to be good; it only made them legalistic. This has some significant implications for the economic results of politics in the world today.

The following discussions assume free markets, where transactions are voluntary and buyers and sellers are free to trade on terms they both find acceptable. Markets, in this sense, are not necessarily physical places, but rather abstract descriptions of systems of voluntary human interaction, simply models to understand the way things work.

Most markets are not totally free. In those that are not fully voluntary, where at least some transactions are coerced, the economic laws still hold, but people's choices are artificially limited, and the results are distorted. They may not be as beneficial as would normally be expected. For instance, in nonfree markets, prices can come about through coercion or government rules, rather than satisfying the needs of buyers and sellers. Some of the other traders may be worse off after the transaction.

Milton Friedman (1912–2006), a Nobel laureate and one of the most influential economists in our time, said that the fundamental ideas in economics could be presented on one sheet of paper, which anyone could understand.[5] There are various versions of this summary, and page 11 is an attempt by this author to summarize them in a form appropriate for the purposes of this book.

The ideas are not original and are not very difficult to comprehend, but there may be some difficulty in overcoming preconceived notions, to open your mind to new ways of looking at things, or overcoming fallacies that you may have learned.

This is not a comprehensive analysis, but rather a concise explanation of the foundations of economic understanding and how they fit with God's truth as revealed in the Bible. Some people may disagree with the importance of the items on the list, for items included or those left out, but few will disagree with the validity of most of the ideas themselves. I hope that the concepts included are adequate to get a cohesive view without being burdensome.

This is, by no means, the only way to interpret economic phenomena. It is, in the author's opinion, a way that ties together the many pieces and avoids the inconsistencies and fallacies inherent in many other approaches to economics. The objective of the following chapters is to support that view, but also to demonstrate

---

[5] Autobiographical essay in *Lives of the Laureates,* edited by William Breit and Roger W. Spencer, (Cambridge, Massachusetts: MIT Press, 1986), p. 91.

that it is an interpretation that is consistent with the word of God and the gospel of Jesus.

2. Economics In One Page

1. **Humans act** because they expect to be better off.

2. **Time** is an element in every decision.

3. **Marginal thinking** - People make decisions at the margin.

4. **Cost** is the trade-off required to satisfy a need.

5. **Demand** tends to increase as prices decrease.

6. **Supply** tends to increase as prices increase.

7. **Price** is a market signal to buyers and sellers.

8. **Division of labor** increases productivity.

9. **Money** is a commodity to enable and enhance trade.

10. **Comparative advantage** helps all those participating.

11. **Profits and wages** arise from satisfying the needs of others.

12. **Profits** direct economic activity to its highest productivity.

13. **Trade and capital** accumulation foster economic progress.

14. **Resources** come from the human mind.

15. **Good intentions** don't equal good results.

3. Human Action

Humans act because they expect to be better off.

For where your treasure is, there will your heart be also.(Mt 6:20)

Jesus' statement above emphasized the importance of right living and right thinking. All of our decisions are made based on what we value in our lives. If we don't value our relationship with God, then our decisions will be made outside that relationship.

Human action is making a decision about how best to satisfy some unmet need, physical, emotional, or spiritual. It is the use of means to attain ends.[6] For example, if you are under a shade tree in the hammock, drowsy and comfortable, you may feel a little thirsty, but decide that you are too comfortable to get up. In the sense of human action that we are talking about, you have acted, even though you didn't move a muscle. You went through the decision-making process, weighed the alternatives, and decided that doing nothing was the best way to act. Not doing anything gave the most satisfying result.

This is very important to understand, because economic decisions are often not apparent to an outside observer. Many economists miss this point, because they hold measurement to be of utmost importance. Not doing anything is generally not measurable and thus, unimportant to them. As Albert Einstein is quoted as saying, however, "Not everything that counts can be counted, and

---

[6] Ludwig Von Mises (1881–1973), *Human Action,* 4th ed., (San Francisco: Fox & Wilkes, 1996), 13.

not everything that can be counted counts." Things that don't happen, or are simply not measurable, are frequently as important as things that do happen with measurable results.

Jesus often talked about the reward for following his way. He was not talking about a worldly reward. "Rejoice and be glad, for great is your reward in heaven." (Mt 5:12) "For if you love those who love you, what reward will you get?" (Mt 5:46) "But when you fast, put oil on your head and wash your face, so that it will not be obvious to men that you are fasting, but only to your Father, who is unseen; and your Father, who sees what is done in secret, will reward you." (Mt 6:17–18) There are twenty five references to "reward" in the New Testament.

People do things because they believe that they will be better off, in some way, after the action. They value things in accordance with how they believe those things will affect their well-being, whether physically, emotionally, or spiritually. This can also be described as self-interest. That sounds like selfishness, and, as such, it is rejected by many people as earthly and unworthy. Even benevolent and altruistic people, however, act because they expect to be better off. They may just think that they will be more pious or more worthy or more socially acceptable because of their actions, but that is using the means of benevolence to attain the ends of heavenly reward and/or good feelings and the esteem of others here and now.

This is not to downplay the importance of charity and kindness or the sincerity of people who display those attributes. It is merely stating the obvious. People act because they expect the result to be better than the prior state of affairs.

This gives rise to another important concept in dealing with human action and relationships: that incentives matter. It seems obvious, but must be stated outright because it is so often ignored by policy makers. People do things a certain way because they believe that they will get the results they are looking for.

When government policies thwart that action, they give rise to incentives to get the results using different means. Over the decades, it can be seen that one government policy gives rise to perverse, unexpected results. They are not necessarily perverse in a moral sense, but rather in the sense that the objective of the policy is perverted. Negative consequences arise that hurt more people than are helped by the original measure. In that case, another policy is implemented to alleviate the negative consequences of the first manipulation, and further perverse results occur.

Clear examples are the prohibition of alcohol from 1920 to 1933 and the war on drugs for the last 35 years, since 1980. They did not reduce alcoholism or drug addiction. These problems were and are unchanged. The results have been, rather, a strengthening of criminal gangs, black markets, extreme violence, restrictions on freedom, militarization of the police, and the making of criminals out of good, ordinary people.

Another familiar and ongoing case is the distortion of agricultural markets through continual tinkering by politicians. As a result of the Agricultural Adjustment Act of the 1930s, millions of livestock animals were killed, millions of bushels of wheat were burned, and millions of acres of cotton were plowed under or otherwise destroyed. Farmers were paid, using taxpayer money, not to grow crops and livestock. The net result was to make food more expensive for all consumers, which, incidentally, included the poor and unemployed. It was especially morally perverse at a time when millions of people were destitute during the Great Depression. Many of the absurd programs from that time are still with us today. Nearly all markets in the United States and other developed countries are now highly regulated, with troublesome effects continually popping up unexpectedly.

Over a period of years, rules are layered on rules, because people react by finding a way to get what they need and want. We now live in an atmosphere where it is very difficult to know the consequences of many actions we take, because the economic incentives have been so distorted. People often act more because of the political consequences than because of the underlying economic reality.

Nobody knows the goals, hopes, dreams, fears, and assumptions about the future of any other person. Even long-time spouses and best friends cannot experience the childhood, adolescence and adulthood of their companions. They may share some common experiences, but most of what the other person thinks arises from the billions of details and experiences of his or her lifetime. There is no objective way to impose good results on a mass of people, because every individual has a different opinion of what good results look like. Everyone shares the same logic, and people make decisions in the same way. They don't, however, share the same values or weigh the good or bad in the same way, not even among those of the same faith or religious background.

Christ offered choices, and still does. He invites people to follow him. We must make that choice every day, but we also must recognize that he offers the same to everyone else. While we are to raise our children and those dependent on us in the way of discipline, he does not call upon us or on politicians to force our neighbors to act as we think they should. He calls on us, rather, to encourage all to know the will of God and follow the laws of creation in all of their actions.

The commandments put strict limits on our authority to violate the rights of others, whether or not they are Christian. By the same token, those rights are the basis of our protection from others. Rights based on the commandments are always a two-way street. As we will see later, good government consists in protecting those rights of each individual to make his or her own choices, limited only by the rights of others.

4. Time

Time is an element in every decision.

"Look" he said, "the sun is still high; it is not time for the flocks to be gathered. Water the sheep and take them back to pasture." (Gn 29:6–8)

When someone makes a decision, there is a specific time frame in mind that helps to determine which option is the most appropriate. Some decisions are made because of the immediate consequences. Snatching a child from out of the path of an oncoming vehicle springs from the absolute necessity of the moment. On the other hand, deciding to save for that same child's college education is a more deliberate choice, taking into consideration the significant length of time until the anticipated benefits of the action are realized.

The economic concept of time value addresses the fact that, in general, a bird in the hand is worth two in the bush, as the old saying goes. Everyone would rather have the benefits of their property immediately rather than having to wait for them until next year. There are good reasons for this. Waiting involves putting off satisfaction to a later date and entails some level of risk that you might not receive the benefit later.

If someone wants to borrow $1,000 for a year, that person has to induce someone else to lend it. The lender has $1,000 in hand now. It is available to do whatever he or she wants with it. Once the money is lent out, not only is it no longer available to satisfy the needs of the lender during the term of the loan, there is some level of risk that the money might not get paid back at all, or only partially paid back.

Interest can be thought of as the price of the inducement to lend. It has further implications, however, because the value of time affects every decision, whether it involves money and interest or not. A head of lettuce is perishable. The decision to buy the lettuce may depend on the timing of when it is to be used. Alternately, you may like having a nice warm house in the winter, but the amount of time that the furnace is cranking out heat may have an impact on other spending decisions, now or in the future.

Time is a factor in all decisions because it involves whether to get satisfaction now or to delay the same or different satisfaction to a later time. Even skipping stones on a nice calm pond is a decision to use the present time for immediate gratification, the good feeling of childish freedom, rather than engaging in some other activity that may give other, future satisfaction.

Profits from business and returns on investments can be thought of as the payback for the inconvenience of doing without the money invested. Entrepreneurs are those people who forgo the immediate benefits of property they own for the potential of greater benefits from running a business. As is readily evident from the number of bankruptcies throughout the years, the benefits don't always appear as expected, but that expectation of future profit motivates people to make the commitment.

Entrepreneurs perform the function of shouldering the burden of uncertainty for their employees and suppliers. Employees provide the services as agreed and get paid in the short term. They do not have to bear the risk that the product may be made obsolete by new competitors or technologies, or that the economy may crumble. Business owners must borrow and make payments to lenders, to employees, and to suppliers, even if not one sale of their products is made.

That certainty of obligations and uncertainty of future returns means that the owners are the residual recipient of the proceeds generated by the business. They get only what's left over after everyone else gets paid. There must be a reasonable expectation that this residual will be great enough not only to compensate for time and effort and to pay back the original money invested in equipment, facilities, and labor, but also to compensate for the possibility that there might be a loss.

Some businesses begin paying back nearly immediately, while others take a very long time to give a return on the investment. As a rule, the greater the risk of loss and the further in the future the expected return, the greater the expected return will need to be in order to induce the investment, whether the investment is a loan to an individual or the multiyear construction of a massive building project.

The risk involved in time arises because of uncertainty. Hurricanes may flatten cities. Borrowers may die or go bankrupt before paying the loan back. An airplane may fall on your house. Terrorists may strike. The list of things that can potentially go wrong is endless. The further into the future the expected outcome lies, the more uncertainty is involved. Generally speaking, the more uncertainty there is, the higher the inducement that is needed to get people to take the risk. Comprehending time value is essential to an understanding of how and why human beings act. It also can lead to a better understanding of incentives and social phenomena.

People have different value systems and their views of time may vary significantly. Some people are very aware of time. It is important to them. They plan their every move and try to wring all they can from the time they have. Others don't value time nearly as much. Things get done when they get to them. If they don't get done then, oh well, life will go on. The choices made by people of those different personality types will tend to be very different, as will the results of those choices.

The more value a person places on his or her time, the higher the price he or she is willing to pay for the things that preserve that time. Bustling business people may pay the high price of an airline ticket in order to save travel time. Poor people may choose a bus ride, even though it takes much longer, because they value the cash they have in their pockets more than the time they have to spend on the bus. Both decisions are rational, based on the assumptions and expectations of the decision makers.

In all cases, however, the value that the individual places on time affects the values placed on all other things, and that influences, consciously or otherwise, every decision made.

5. Marginal Thinking

People make decisions at the margin.

The foolish ones said to the wise, "Give us some of your oil, our lamps are going out." "No," they replied, "there may not be enough for both us and you. Instead, go to those who sell oil and buy some for yourselves." (Mt 25:8–9)

The wise ones in the parable were not unduly selfish. Under other circumstances they might have shared, but not on this occasion, because the foolish ones did not plan ahead and the limited amount on hand would not be enough for everyone. The value of that small amount of oil was very high. If their oil ran out, they would be left behind.

When people make a choice of which action to take, they necessarily weigh the costs and benefits of the alternatives. When they decide, however, they don't take into account the cost or benefit of every quantity of every good. They decide using only the quantities that are relevant to the decision. The next units produced, purchased, or consumed are all that generally matter to decision makers.

The value of a jug of water is not based on all of the water in the world. Each person values water based on his or her particular circumstances at the time. If someone has plenty of water for all of his or her needs, that person will not place a high value on the next cup of water. A person whose life is endangered by lack of water places a very high value on the next cup. This can help to explain what some consider a paradox. Why is it that water, which is essential to life, without which no person can live, has a low price, whereas diamonds, which are typically considered frivolous, unnecessary luxuries, carry a very high price tag?

To understand it, imagine yourself standing by a stream of water, and you can drink as much as you want. You have an expensive diamond ring and someone standing with you has a jug of water. If that person offers you the jug of water for that ring, it is not likely that you will take the offer. You don't value the water very highly because the next unit cannot offer you much additional satisfaction.

Now imagine yourself out in the desert. You have been there for days and are dehydrated with no water available. If you come across the person with the jug of water now, it would be much more likely that you would be willing to trade the ring for the life-saving water. The value you place on the next unit, the marginal unit, is very high because it will satisfy a need that is great. If the person trades with you, it is because he or she values the ring more than the water.

The value that an individual places on a particular good is based on the next relevant unit of the good or service. The decision is made at the margin and reflects the additional satisfaction that the units bring to the individual. The next, or marginal, unit is the only quantity that is relevant for decision making.

The value that any person associates with a particular good or service is subjective. It is based on that person's circumstances and expectations. A change in those circumstances will change the value that this individual places on the item.

Another example might serve to illustrate the idea. Suppose that you go to the store and see that lettuce is on sale at half price. You remember that you already have lettuce at home so, even though it is relatively inexpensive, you decide not to get it. If, the next day, you find out that you are hosting a dinner at your house and there will not be enough lettuce, you may go back to the store and buy three heads at full price. It doesn't seem to make sense that you would buy more lettuce at a higher price, but the value that you place on those particular heads of lettuce at that particular time is based on the value that you place on a successful dinner party.

The importance of this idea will become more apparent when we look at how prices are determined by supply and demand.

6. Cost

Cost is the trade-off required to satisfy a need.

Again, the kingdom of heaven is like a merchant looking for fine pearls. When he found one of great value, he went away and sold everything he had and bought it. (Mt 13:45)

People have wants, needs, desires, and goals, and they seek effective means to satisfy them. Cost is often measured in terms of price, and we typically think of price in terms of money. In a more general sense, however, there is a cost for everything that we decide to do or not do. It can be in terms of time or the other things we cannot do, in terms of pain or hardship, or in terms of what other goods we have to give up in order to attain the good we desire. It is an idea that Jesus used very effectively at various times, that of counting the cost. "The kingdom of heaven is like a treasure hidden in a field. When a man found it, he hid it again, and then in his joy went and sold all he had and bought that field." (Mt 13:44) Jesus was explaining through a parable that the cost of following him is very dear.

In a more mundane sense, trade, markets, selling, and buying were natural processes that people took for granted from the earliest biblical times. People took cost into account every day. That is why they could relate to Jesus' parable. Today, our physical world looks very different from the things they encountered 2,000 years ago, but we still count the cost in the same way. We ask, consciously or unconsciously, "What do I have to give up so that I can get what I desire?"

Opportunity cost is the recognition that there are certain things that are mutually exclusive. There are only 24 hours in a day. If you spend 8 or 10 hours per day developing your skills to be a world-class concert pianist, those hours are no longer available to develop the skills needed to be an Olympic champion athlete. The opportunity cost of one course of action is whatever else you wanted to do or have, but had to give up in order to get what you wanted more. It is the value of the most highly valued alternative.

I learned a word back in college days that stuck with me all through the years. That word is TINSTAAFL. It is an acronym for "There is no such thing as a free lunch." It has to do with the idea of cost, but deals with a fallacy that often distorts the decision-making process for individuals and political leaders. The fundamental principle is that everything has a cost.

If someone takes you out to lunch and pays the tab, the lunch was free for you, but it wasn't free. Your friend bears the cost rather than you. If the restaurant owner tells your friend that the meals are on the house, the restaurant owner bears the cost, instead of your friend. When real resources, including time, are used up, there is a real cost. Someone ultimately bears that cost. They have used up the opportunity to use the resources for alternative choices.

The idea of counting the cost that Jesus talked about had nothing to do with money, but rather what you have to give up, the idea of opportunity cost. If you act in one way, you must give up the benefits of acting another way. What you give up is the cost of the lost opportunity. That concept is central to our decision-making every day.

This idea applies to government programs as well as dinners out. Someone pays for everything. You may be getting a benefit, but if you are not bearing the cost, someone else is. That someone is the present taxpayer, future taxpayers, or all consumers when the tax takes the form of monetary inflation. In all of these cases, forcing the cost of a benefit that you receive onto the shoulders of someone else is a form of theft. Trillions of dollars of government debt arises from borrowing money for present consumption. That debt must be paid back by taking money from the pockets of other Americans now or those of our grandchildren and great-grandchildren. It is the immoral transfer of wealth from those who ultimately pay to those who get the present benefit.

Jesus calls on us to count the cost, to know the implications of our actions, and to make decisions with full knowledge and understanding. He also calls on us to shoulder our own burdens, to pay the price, and to live up to our obligations. For some people, those burdens are very heavy, and he also calls us to help ease those burdens on the poor and less fortunate. Throughout the bible, God called His people to have compassion and to help those in need. He never asks us, however, to steal from others for our good deeds.

7. Demand

Demand tends to increase as prices decrease.

If he cannot afford a lamb, he is to bring two doves or two young pigeons to the LORD as a penalty for his sin—one for a sin offering and the other for a burnt offering. (Lv 5:6–8)

When something has a high price, fewer people will be able to afford it, as illustrated in the verse from Leviticus. Doves or pigeons were substituted for the lamb. That substitution decreased the number of lambs that buyers were both willing and able to buy. Whether or not anyone views sacrificial animals as an adequate substitute for true repentance and a clean heart, as an economic example, the high price of lambs decreased the quantity demanded.

In a modern economic sense, "the market" is an abstract idea that describes the relationships between supply, demand, and prices. It is a way to understand reality. There are, indeed, particular physical markets, places where goods are bought and sold, but the markets that are described in economics are only representations of what happens in any market, whether it is a building at a particular location or a system of trading of goods over a wide area. The model of a market is a way to present concepts that make it easier to grasp the essentials of human interaction.

In economics, demand is the relationship between the prices of an item and the quantities that willing and able buyers are prepared to purchase. It is a set of values that describes a dynamic process. Demand is not what people say they want, or feel they should have, but rather, it is the actual quantities of product that buyers would purchase at each price in a particular market at a given point in time. It is a reflection of the wide range of opportunity costs that different individuals face. Using our travel example, as the price, or cost, of airline tickets decreases, more people would think that the value of the time they save is worth the money they need to pay. The number of airline tickets sold generally increases as the price decreases.

It has often been said that a picture is worth a thousand words, and in discussing these ideas, that is particularly true. While charts and graphs have been kept to a minimum, I hope that the diagrams presented on the following pages will help to get the ideas across in an efficient manner that makes them easy to remember.

It is important to recognize that these graphs are merely logical ways to present ideas. Because society, the economy, and the world are constantly changing, the actual demand is also constantly changing. The picture does, however, help to firmly establish logical relationships.

If we think of our everyday lives, we can determine the relationship between price and the quantity demanded. We looked previously at the idea of marginal thinking, the understanding that all decisions are made at the margin. We also discussed the concept that everyone values the various goods and services differently, based on his or her particular circumstances and expectations. So, for a particular market, for a specific good, there may be some people who are willing to buy even at a high price, because it meets some important need or desire for them. There are others who would only buy it if the price was very low. The marginal value that it offers them does not offset the opportunity cost of what they have to give up in order to get it.

In general, the lower the price, the more of a good or service that people will buy. Retailers recognize this relationship and take advantage of it every time they have a sale. When they want to move a higher quantity of an item, they offer various types of discounts or incentives, which have the effect of lowering the price.

They know that, at a lower price, people will generally buy more.

Think about the day after Thanksgiving, known as Black Friday, a day for shoppers. People flock to the stores because of all the fantastic bargains they expect to get. Lower prices increase the number of items sold. It makes sense, based on what we know about our own habits and preferences. The logic of human action fits the reality of human action.

In the graph of diagram 1, the horizontal axis represents the quantity of an item demanded. Quantity increases as we move to the right. The vertical axis represents the price. The higher we go up the scale, the higher the price.

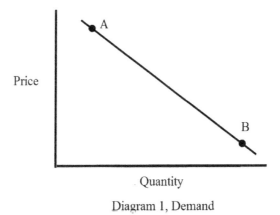

Diagram 1, Demand

As a rule, the higher the price, the lower the quantity of the item that will be demanded, because the higher price excludes those who value the item less. On the graph, point A represents a high price of the item. The point will appear somewhere in the upper left hand corner of the graph. Point B represents a low price for the item. The quantity demanded will be high. It will fall somewhere in the lower right portion of the diagram. The line that passes through those points represents all of the various combinations of price and quantity along the scales.

In reality, the graph for any particular item is not likely a straight line, and the shape and slope may be very different for different types of products. It does make sense, however, that the line or curve will slope downward to the right in most cases, with only very minor exceptions. It is generally called a demand curve.

The whole curve can move to the right or left, or change shape or slope, depending on many interrelated factors. There may be new competing products that reduce the demand for the old one. The demographic content of a population may change, which affects the number of potential buyers for the product. There may be a natural disaster that instantly creates a massive demand, or destroys it, for a particular item or service.

Entrepreneurs, those who attempt to provide the good or service that is demanded, need to take potential changes in demand into account in planning, and those who are the best at predicting future demand are the ones who will be in the position to satisfy the demand better than competitors. Those who anticipate the future better are usually rewarded with a higher profit.

8. Supply

Supply tends to increase as prices increase.

She sets about her work vigorously; her arms are strong for her tasks. She sees that her trading is profitable, and her lamp does not go out at night. (Prv 31:17–18)

The Law of Supply can be understood as: That which is profitable is copied and repeated. That which is unprofitable is not. The verse from Proverbs above describes a woman of noble character who is diligent and active. Because she sees that her trading of the things she makes is profitable, "her lamp does not go out at night." That is, she spends more time making those things that will bring benefit to her and her family. Other people, on seeing her success, would likely also do some of the things she does. Were the activity not profitable, neither she nor anyone else would continue doing it. It is important to remember that, in this context, profits can mean more than money profits. The joy of doing certain activities can sometimes be enough profit to make it worthwhile. Amateur performers, hospital candy stripers and millions of other volunteer workers get what might be termed "psychic profit", and happily perform their duties with no monetary consideration.

In general terms, the quantity of an item that suppliers are willing and able to offer to a given market varies with the price of the item. All other things being equal, the quantity supplied increases as the market price increases. This also can be represented on a simple graph as a supply curve. The exact shape of the line or curve is, again, not knowable, but we can deduce the general relationship because it arises from what we know about human logic, similar to the demand curve.

With a very low price, few entrepreneurs will attempt to produce or supply the good or the service. Since business people also have opportunity costs for their time, capital, and money, they will avoid those businesses that return too little in relation to what they have to give up. It will be much more difficult to make a profit at the lower price and they will produce fewer of less profitable items. On the other hand, if an item is very profitable, or in other words, the amount they give up is considerably less than what they get, there is a significant incentive to provide more. New suppliers will also be drawn into a profitable market. Thus, a higher price will tend to lead to an increase in the quantity supplied.

As with demand, the price does not necessarily mean only the money cost of an item. There are many other factors involved, including the entrepreneur's family time and the level of personal satisfaction or enjoyment experienced by the business person. It is, however, relatively easy to depict prices as money prices.

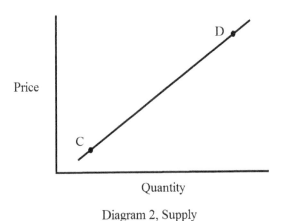

Diagram 2, Supply

We can draw a supply curve, similar to the demand curve above, but it will be just the inverse. Again, it is logical that it should be this way in all but exceptional cases. With diagram 2, a low price will be accompanied by a low quantity supplied. It can be represented by a point C in the lower left corner of the diagram. A higher price will be accompanied by a larger quantity supplied, represented by a point D in the upper right hand corner.

It is possible, and even probable, that, like the demand curve, the whole supply curve will shift positions and change shape over time. Various factors can affect the curve, such as new competing products, fluctuations in production costs, legislation, and demographic changes. The shift reflects the new incentives to the producers and the new reality of the relationship between quantity and prices. In nearly all cases, however, the quantity of a particular item that is supplied tends to increase with higher prices.

There may be some confusion regarding this principle because, historically, inflation adjusted prices of goods have declined dramatically, even as the supply has increased over time. The computer is a familiar example. When they were first manufactured, they were extremely expensive, and only large corporations could buy them. In the course of several decades, the price of computers has dropped to the point where most families can afford them, and many millions are sold each year. It seems to run counter to the Law of Supply. The computers purchased in the present consumer markets, however, are very different products, with different materials, production processes and costs than the early, high-cost models for business. Rather than being a refutation of the Law of Supply, it is a description of competition and how markets develop to the benefit of consumers.

When a new product is introduced, the costs are high, and few suppliers are capable of producing it. The supply is low and the selling price is high. At that point in time, though, the higher the price and the resulting profits, the greater is the incentive to produce more; the law of supply holds sway. As time goes on, manufactures become more efficient and profitable. As more firms attempt to capture some of the market and profits, new, cost-effective materials, processes, and inventions reduce production costs. Competition in the industry forces prices down.

The competitive pressure that drives costs down over a period of time is a different phenomenon than the relationship between price and supply in a particular market at a point in time. Competition and the Law of Supply work together, dynamically affecting prices and supplies over time. Both have an effect and both have rational, but very different, explanations. Competition and development of markets will be dealt with in more depth in the chapter on Profits (pages 56-59) and the chapter on Trade and Capital (pages 60-69.)

9. Prices

Price is a market signal to buyers and sellers.

But he answered, "You give them something to eat." They said to him, "That would take eight months worth of a man's wages. Are we to go and spend that much on bread and give it to them?" (Mk 6:37)

In the reference above, the price of a large quantity of bread was stated in terms of the portion of a man's annual wage that would be required to feed all of the people. Jesus' request was meant to impress the apostles to trust him and to believe that God will provide. Behind the scene, however, we can understand that the world of that time worked in a remarkably similar way to the world of our time. Bread had a price. It was a valuable commodity, and people paid money for it because it satisfied a want.

Price is arguably the most important idea in all of economics, because it serves as a signal for all people in the market, whether they are buyers or sellers, demanders or suppliers. The market is the communication medium for the signal. When buyers walk away from a deal, it is a signal to the seller that the price is too high. When a seller walks away from the deal, it is a signal to the buyer that the offered price is too low. A sale only results when the price is high enough for the seller and low enough for the buyer.

The monetary price of the good or service in a free market results from an interaction between the demand and supply relationships. At low prices, lots of people will be willing and able to buy, but few sellers will be willing and able to sell. At a high price, there will be few buyers, but many sellers.

If you overlay the graphs of supply and demand, as in diagram 3, you will find that the curves intersect at some point.

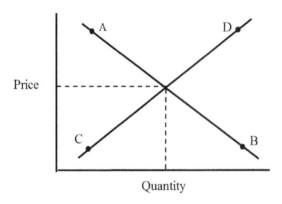

Diagram 3, Supply & Demand

That is the point where the quantity supplied and the quantity demanded are equal. That point in the market for the particular good or service is considered an equilibrium position, the point toward which the market will tend to move. It is the price at which all goods will clear the market.

There never will be a perfect equilibrium at any time for any market because conditions are dynamic. Seasons change, disasters happen, children grow up to be teenage eating machines, people die, and on and on. The market is constantly changing. The price in a free market, however, will tend to increase or decrease toward the point where the number of willing and able buyers approximately matches the number of willing and able sellers. That is the market price, an equilibrium point at which there are neither shortages nor gluts of goods or services.

There are reasons for this based on what each of us knows about how we, as human beings, act. We, in our highly developed economy, still use the same thought processes in our relationships, our trading, and our buying as those people two thousand or even six thousand years ago. That is why we can relate to the stories of the Bible. The people of those times were human beings as we are human beings. They displayed the same human logic and emotions that we do today. When the woman poured expensive perfume on Jesus' head, some of the disciples were indignant. They said: "This perfume could have been sold at a high price, and the money given to the poor." (Mt 26:8) They recognized the significance of prices in their actions. Jesus, however, pointed out that there are things that are more valuable than money.

People in the business of supplying goods are at the mercy of the customer. Customers in a free market will not buy if they think the price is too high, and there is nothing the business owners can do to force them. If the business owners are fortunate enough or had enough foresight to be in a market with a large and growing demand, the prices will tend to be higher, as there are too few competitors trying to supply all of the potential customers.

On the other hand, if a market is declining, the suppliers will likely have to deal with low prices, as supply outstrips the demand. Fewer suppliers will be able to keep their costs below the decreased price and some will have to leave the market.

It is relevant to our later discussions to understand clearly the implications of prices on shortages or gluts of goods and services. Because nature and human society are dynamic, there are and always will be circumstances that disrupt what people come to accept as normal market conditions. A hurricane can create an immediate shortage of drinkable water and building supplies. A health scare, true or imagined, can cause a sudden rapid disappearance of demand for a given item believed to be dangerous. These are simply examples, but the possibilities for disruptive circumstances are almost limitless.

In a case where shortages or gluts are particularly severe or last for more than a short time, that is evidence that prices are being artificially held below or above the market price by some outside force, such as government regulation or threats of prosecution. The further the prices are held below or above the market price, the more severe the shortage or the glut will be.

Market Shortages

Diagram 4 below depicts what happens when price controls artificially hold the price below the level where the quantity demanded equals the quantity supplied.

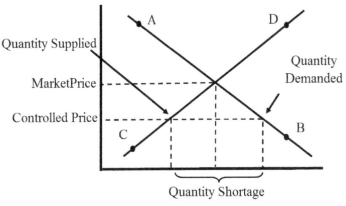

Diagram 4, Shortage In Market

When the legal price is held below the market price, it encourages buyers to demand more. Cheapness is an incentive to buy. On the diagram, the quantity demanded is to the right of what it would be at the market clearing price. At the same time, the low price induces suppliers to supply less to the market for the reasons explored previously. Cheapness reduces profitability, which in turn, reduces the incentive to supply and sell. The quantity supplied will therefore be less than the quantity demanded. This phenomenon happens whenever prices are capped below the market price. The

1970's gasoline price controls in America caused severe shortages and long waiting lines for gasoline. Price-gouging threats from government officials are a form of price controls, and suppliers keep prices artificially low, in spite of greatly increased demand for the product. Those price-gouging threats caused shortages and hampered reconstruction of New Orleans years after the damage was done by Hurricane Katrina. The further from the market price the controlled price gets, the more severe the shortage will be, as the supply and demand diverge further and further.

Market Gluts

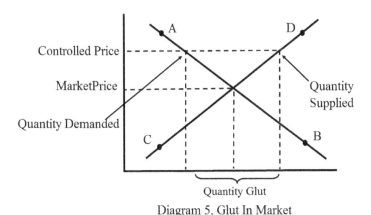

Diagram 5, Glut In Market

Diagram 5 shows the case of price controls that artificially hold the price above the market price.

When the price is held above the market price, the opposite incentives occur. Suppliers are encouraged to supply more of the product than customers are willing and able to buy. Unemployment arises when labor prices are held above the market price for a particular skill. The high price can result from minimum-wage law, collective bargaining, or from the resistance of individual workers to work at lower wages. More striking examples are the severe gluts in agricultural products when government subsidies encourage production in excess of demand. The further above the market price that the controlled price rises, the more severe the glut of goods will be, as supply and demand diverge, continuing in the opposite directions.

This analysis can be used to understand a wide range of economic phenomena, where people are the victims of political ideology that ignores economic reality. The problems cannot be solved by mere political will, but rather, only by submitting to the immutable laws of God's ordered world, the laws of economics that determine market outcomes. Section 3 will deal more specifically with the implications of policy decisions on supply and demand, gluts and shortages.

The Second Book of Kings chapters 6 and 7 describe the situation of the city of Samaria, as it was under siege. The siege is a tactic of warfare where a city is cut off from all outside sources of food and water. The idea is to starve the city into surrender. In Samaria, the supply of food had dwindled to such a point that demand was extremely high relative to the very small amount available. A donkey's head, not the most appetizing or nutritious part, was sold as food and brought an extremely high price, as did seed pods and anything else that could be eaten. At the height of the famine, God told Elisha that the price of flour and barley would sell for normal prices the very next day.

As the story unfolds, God drove the Aramean army to flee for their lives, and they left everything behind, including all of their food. It immediately became plentiful for the residents of the city, and the prices rapidly decreased, as God had told Elisha. The increased supply of food caused a more normal equilibrium level, and the prices dropped to a fraction of what they were just the previous day. When food is plentiful, nobody is going to pay a high price for very undesirable animal parts.

The Bible was not written as a treatise on economics, but it does demonstrate that, even in ancient times, human phenomena were guided by economic laws. When demand is very high relative to the supply, the price has to be high. When the demand is very low relative to the supply, the price must be low. While God's power can influence events, his laws still govern our lives.

10. Division of Labor

The division of labor increases productivity

If the whole body were an eye, where would the sense of hearing be? If the whole body were an ear, where would the sense of smell be? But in fact God has arranged the parts in the body, every one of them, just as he wanted them to be. If they were all one part, where would the body be? As it is, there are many parts, but one body. (1Cor12:17–20)

Society in the time of Jesus was quite primitive compared to our modern society. It was primarily agrarian, with a large portion of the population working the land as farmers of some sort. Even in those times, however, it is clear that some people specialized in the work that they did. Joseph was a carpenter. The apostles were fishermen, tax collectors, and had other occupations. The gospels refer to innkeepers, shepherds, builders, merchants, and so forth.

Every society that rises above mere subsistence agriculture or nomadic wandering does so because people begin to specialize. It is an obvious fact of life that everyone can't be good at everything. The very act of concentrating on one skill necessarily means that there are fewer hours in a day, week, year, and lifetime to devote to something else. The concept of opportunity cost prevails in careers also. The limited number of hours in a day provides an absolute limit to the things people can do. The choice of one career comes at the cost of another, different career.

Some people have innate characteristics that make them suitable for success in different endeavors. A three hundred pound muscular hulk will certainly not make a very good jockey for horse racing, but might be a very good candidate for offensive lineman of a football team. The characteristics necessary to be a good surgeon generally mean that you don't typically find surgeons who are also professional boxers.

In general, the higher the level of skill necessary for a given endeavor, the more time it takes to develop that skill. You can't be a world-class figure skater and a world class-concert pianist. They are generally exclusive of each other because each takes many hours of dedication every day. Being world class at any endeavor drastically reduces the amount of time any individual is able to devote to any other activity.

A professional pianist cannot eat music, however. Like the rest of us, he or she must eat food. How can people who know only how to perform a limited specialty service, such as piano concerts, survive when human needs, such as food, shelter, and clothing, press upon them as upon every other human being? The answer is, of course, that people trade. The pianist trades entertainment services for food, clothing, vehicles, computers, and homes.

They are able to trade for these things because other people specialize in other professions, crafts, and occupations. These other people spend their time developing a high level of skill in engineering, electronics, carpentry, retailing, farming, and so on They are able to produce more by specializing so that they can trade their excess to others, who also produce in excess of what they need.

It is fascinating to watch professionals do their work. While modern carpentry may not be as fun and exciting to watch as professional basketball, it can be an amazing performance as well, when in the presence of a professional. There is no wasted movement, no wasted time. They have the right skills and the right tools for the job. It is a wonder how they can do what they do in the short amount of time they take.

Because highly skilled people give more, more entertainment, more houses built, more plumbing installed, or more successful knee surgeries, their time becomes more valuable and they get more in trade.

A diesel mechanic is able to do something very valuable, but there are only so many diesel engines that he or she can fix for himself or herself. Each successive engine repaired has a lesser value to that person from the perspective of personal use. A farmer produces much more food than he or she can use. For the farmer personally, the marginal value of the food in excess of what can be consumed by the family is very low. The farmer, however, is willing to pay a high price for the next unit of diesel service so that the tractor can be put back into production. The mechanic is able to pay for food because he has the skill to fix tractors and other equipment.

The farmer is willing to pay the diesel mechanic because he is more productive being a farmer than fixing tractor engines. Both the farmer and the mechanic produce more of an item or service than they can use. They willingly and voluntarily pay for the other because the cost incurred is less than the opportunity cost of doing it themselves.

Jesus used the parable of the wise and foolish builders. (Mt 7:24–27) Two men built houses, one on a solid foundation and the other on sand. The primary lesson was for us to build our lives on the foundation of faith in God. The story, in itself, however, is the recognition that results matter. Going through the motions doesn't necessarily give the good result. The builder who took care to do it right was rewarded when the storm came and his house was preserved. The foolish builder, who did not take care, lost his house in the storm. Actions have implications.

The wise builder, whose house survived the storm, could use his available time after the storm for other productive things, whereas the foolish builder was forced to use his time to rebuild, because he did not take care originally. People who use their skills wisely can preserve extra time that is available for doing everything else that they want to do, including being more productive and earning more or having the capacity to spend time with family, in leisure activities or being charitable.

As we will see, this is an important insight into how societies develop. The less time spent producing the bare essentials, the more time that is left over to increase personal well-being and prosperity, both for the individual and for the collection of individuals known as society.

11. Comparative Advantage

Comparative Advantage Helps All Those Participating.

Then they gave money to the masons and carpenters, and gave food and drink and oil to the people of Sidon and Tyre, so that they would bring cedar logs by sea from Lebanon to Joppa, as authorized by Cyrus king of Persia. (Ezr 3:6–8)

Comparative advantage is related to the division of labor in that it has to do with people, organizations, and even entire geographic regions, utilizing specialized skills or resources. As indicated in the verse above, Tyre and Sidon were known for their great sea ports and trade with distant areas. That was what they were best at. Comparative advantage is distinct, however, because it allows us to understand how every person, every organization, and every region can progress at the same time through trade, even if one individual or organization or region is better at doing everything.

Division of labor demonstrates that people can be more productive if they specialize. What happens when one country is better than every other country at every single thing, or one person is better at everything than anyone else? Does that mean that they shouldn't trade with anyone, that they should be self-sufficient? In every case, though they may have an absolute advantage over everyone else, they don't have the same relative advantage for all skills and industries. In some areas they may be ten times as productive. In other areas, they may be only slightly more productive.

This can be illustrated with a simple example. A brain surgeon may be very skillful at keeping medical records, in fact, twice as productive as anyone else. Because brain surgery is a very high-value skill, five or even ten times the value may be produced by practicing surgery than by keeping medical records. The comparative advantage in surgery is larger than for medical records. That person would be better off performing surgeries and letting someone else keep the records.

The medical-records specialist, on the other hand, would starve trying to be a surgeon. People are only going to trust the care of their brain to someone who has had special training and experience in that field. The physician maximizes the value provided by concentrating on surgery. The records specialist maximizes the value produced by concentrating on medical records.

Say the physician can charge $200 an hour as a surgeon and the market rate for medical-records specialist time is $20 per hour. For every hour the surgeon spends keeping medical records, he loses $180 in potential net gain, assuming his services are enough in demand to keep a full schedule. It makes sense for him to hire someone to do something that he himself can do even better, because the comparative advantage is in performing operations.

The same probably holds true for CEOs of major corporations and floor sweepers. The executive may be an excellent, energetic, productive floor sweeper, but his or her comparative advantage is in running multi-billion-dollar businesses. The floor sweeper probably doesn't have to worry about competition for his job from the executive. I am sure that most CEOs are happy to trade with another person to provide the service. By the same token, it is unlikely that any typical person would be willing to do what most of the top CEOs had to do to get where they are.

Nations and large geographic regions each have particular sets of skills and characteristics that allow them to compete in open trade on the world market. A developing country may not have any absolute advantage in any industry, but it still makes sense for it to trade with others and for others to trade with it.

While producers in developing countries may not be able to manufacture woolen sweaters any more efficiently than those in another country, if that is where their comparative advantage lies, then it makes sense for them to concentrate on making sweaters and trade for the things for which they have a lesser advantage. They maximize value for themselves by making sweaters. It would likely make no sense for them to make their own computers or to manufacture automobiles if they could buy them from a company in another country cheaper than they could make them.

The leaders of many contemporary developing countries have the false notion that their country must be self-sufficient, and that they should shield all trades and industries from international competition through trade protections. They have some of the highest tariff rates in the world. Rather than helping their people, however, the net effect of the protectionism is a significant reduction of the value that their workers can produce under open trade as opposed to maximizing their comparative advantage through expanded import and export.

In all cases, people, organizations, and regions are better off if they concentrate on the things in which they create the most value. A developing country trading with an advanced country is very similar to the medical-records specialist trading with the surgeon. Both parties are more productive by doing things that maximize their comparative advantage.

While many geographic areas have the potential ability to be self-sufficient, by doing so they cannot take advantage of the benefits of expanding comparative advantage to cover a wider area. All developed countries have an active trade with other geographic areas. That trade is good for all those involved, because it allows people and regions to specialize in products and services where they can produce the most value overall. It also allows them to meet their other needs at a lower cost and with a greater variety.

12. Money

Money is a commodity to enable and enhance trade.

When the amount had been determined, they gave the money to the men appointed to supervise the work on the temple. With it they paid those who worked on the temple of the LORD—the carpenters and builders, the masons and stonecutters. They purchased timber and dressed stone for the repair of the temple of the LORD, and met all the other expenses of restoring the temple. (2 Kgs 12:10–12)

A pianist doesn't play his or her piano for a farmer in exchange for a side of beef, at least directly. The price of a steer probably does not equal the price of a concert ticket, and even if it did, the pianist does not need hundreds of pounds of meat.

The system of indirect exchange with money was referred to even in the book of Genesis, and it has developed over time to meet the needs of trade that arose as more and more people specialized. It was a solution to the particular problems of barter exchange, the direct exchange of goods without money. Money itself is only a commodity that is used to convey value from one person to another.

Money arises spontaneously from a market system as a result of the desire for trade. In prison camps, money will arise in the form of cigarettes or some other good that the prisoners value. Even those who don't smoke will take the cigarettes in trade, because they can be traded for other things that they do want and need.

Money has developed into different forms over the millennia of human civilization, but the essential characteristic of money is that its value is rooted in the value of goods that it can purchase. The more valuable the things that money can buy, the more valuable the money is. Money is less valuable when it takes more monetary units to buy a set of goods. Modern paper money had its foundation in the value of gold and silver, which were the choices for indirect exchange because of the qualities of divisibility, durability, and usefulness.

Nowadays, paper money is not backed by gold, silver, or any other type of commodity. It is fiat money, that which is created by government fiat or command. It is money because legal-tender laws prohibit other forms of money from competing with the government monopoly on the money supply. The laws require people to take the fiat money in payment of debts. The money is a piece of paper or a bank accounting unit that has value only because others will take it in trade for things of value.

Modern money is made of coins and bills of various denominations, but, much more importantly, it is made up of deposits at banks. Checking and savings accounts are very convenient ways of storing and dispensing money as it is needed. The bank promises to pay immediately whatever you direct them to, up to the amount that you have deposited.

Money prices for goods are determined by the relationship of the supply of money to the goods and services that are available in the economy. W. M. Curtiss gave a good analogy of prices in his 1952 essay entitled *Price Supports*: "Prices of goods and services may be compared with water in a lake. Ripples and waves on the surface of the lake correspond to the prices of individual commodities. They rise and fall in varying degrees depending on supply and demand conditions for each commodity, even though the overall level of the lake may not change. The level of the lake rises and falls because of what happens at the inlet and outlet."[7]

---

[7] W. M. Curtiss, "Price Supports," In *Essays on Liberty,* ed. Leonard Read, (Irvington-On-Hudson: The Foundation For Economic Education, Inc.), 128.

Using Mr. Curtiss's analogy, the general price level has nothing to do with individual prices. Individual prices are but waves on the lake. When prices rise in general, it is due to an increase in the money supply, much as the level of the lake increases with an increase in the supply of water.

The price relationships of all of the various goods and services in an economy are constantly changing, depending on the circumstances at the time. With a constant money supply, the general price level will remain fairly constant, much as the lake remains at the same level. If the price of one item increases, the price of other items must decrease to adjust, just as a wave has a crest and a trough.

To understand price relationships, let us first look at prices in terms of nonmonetary goods. The price of a good or service is the ratio of what you give to what you get. If you are willing to trade one pizza for two grapefruit, your cost of the grapefruit is ½ pizza each. The cost of the pizza is 2 grapefruit. One party buys grapefruit with pizza, or sells pizza for grapefruit. The other party buys pizza with grapefruit or sells grapefruit for pizza. Both are buyers and both are sellers.

If there was suddenly a bumper crop of grapefruit and the quantity available was doubled with no change in the demand for it, the price of each individual grapefruit would likely decline in relation to pizza. Rather than two grapefruit to buy a pizza, it may now take four. The price of pizza would be four grapefruit, but the price of grapefruit would be $1/4^{th}$ of a pizza.

It may seem a little cumbersome to think through it, but it is important and worthwhile to understand the nonmonetary prices to understand money. Money is merely another commodity that has certain characteristics that make it valuable for trade. If we substitute dollars for grapefruit, we can do a similar analysis. The pizza buyer is selling dollars for pizza. The pizza seller is buying dollars with pizza. When pizza can be traded for $2, the price of pizza is $2, but the price of a dollar in terms of pizza is ½ pizza per dollar. If the money supply is doubled, other things being the same, the price of pizza may increase to, say, four dollars. This means that the price of dollars, in terms of pizza is now $1/4^{th}$ pizza. Pizza is now more expensive in terms of dollars.

As the supply of money increases, the amount of pizza that each money unit can buy decreases, similar to the case with grapefruit. This increase in money prices is commonly thought of as inflation, the popular definition. A truer definition of inflation, however, is the increase in the supply of money. The result of that increase is that the general price level increases. More dollars are needed to purchase a given set of goods. This has important implications as we will see in section 3 under the heading "Money and Inflation."

Money is important to the development of societies, because it facilitates trade, and trade is the only way to take full advantage of the benefits of the division of labor and comparative advantage. It is also important because it is all–pervasive, and there are so many profound effects on market participants and the goods and services they trade. Since, in most modern nations, the government has monopoly power over the provision of money, the government has a grave responsibility to its citizens to manage money well, a responsibility mostly forsaken, to the detriment of the citizens.

13. Profits and Wages

Profits and wages arise from satisfying the needs of others.

A generous man will prosper; he who refreshes will himself be refreshed. (Prv 11:25)

We have seen that people produce value by the things that they do. The division of labor enables each individual to produce more value by specializing and focusing efforts on a limited set of skills. By specializing, he or she can produce more of an excess of valuable products beyond what he or she can personally use. The benefits of the division of labor can only be realized, however, by trading with other individuals who also create an excess in some other area. The farmer creates value by growing agricultural products, the carpenter creates value by building things.

Trade, whether direct or indirect, enables the farmer to use the value he created to purchase needed carpenter services. It also allows the carpenter to use the value he created to purchase needed food. The value that one person creates does not come at the expense of another. It is, rather, additive. Both are better off if they increase value to the maximum extent that they can.

Trade arises from the fact that the farmer needs what the carpenter creates and the carpenter needs what the farmer creates. If the carpenter does not do what the farmer needs, or does it with such a poor quality that the farmer can do it more efficiently himself, then the farmer will not trade with the carpenter. Trade occurs in a free market only by satisfying the needs of others.

Let's say the farmer wants to keep his costs low and decides to grow ragweed, because it is so easy to cultivate. He may be a very

53

good ragweed farmer; as a matter of fact, he may be the best, most efficient ragweed producer in the world. The chances are, however, that our farmer friend will not fare too well. There is not much of a market for ragweed, outside of antihistamine-testing labs. The farmer, though he is a knowledgeable, careful, competent producer, is not producing a product that many people are likely to need or to want or to be willing to buy.

On the other hand, the farmer may grow a delicate crop that is rare, is extremely expensive to nurture, and requires a massive capital investment and very specialized knowledge. If the crop is something that people will buy, like orchids and roses, the farmer might make a very good profit, because the market supports higher prices for things that are highly valued.

Wages are, in their essence, a form of profit. Wages result from selling personal services, much the same as profits arise from selling goods. If a worker has developed a valuable skill, he or she will be able to sell that skill to an employer or client for a significant amount of money. Other skills that are easier to acquire, or jobs requiring very little skill, will generally command a much lower price.

People generally take the easy way first. The easier the skill is to develop, the more competitors there will be for those jobs. Nuclear physicists generally don't have a high level of competition, even though there is a good market for the skill, because it is so difficult and time-consuming to get there. The income for nuclear physicists is, understandably, much higher than that of a floor sweeper. They provide valuable services that few competitors are willing and able to provide.

In all cases in a free market, profits and wages come from supplying the needs of others. Whether you are a farmer or carpenter, a physicist or floor sweeper, a butcher, baker, or candlestick maker, you will generally be rewarded in relation to the amount of value you create, value that you can trade to meet the needs of others.

14. Profits

Profits direct economic activity to its highest productivity.

The plans of the diligent lead to profit as surely as haste leads to poverty. (Prv 21:5)

Profit can be monetary, but it can also be purely emotional or spiritual, as when Jesus said, "For what shall it profit a man if he gain the whole world, and lose his own soul?" (Mk 8:36)[8] Profit can be thought of as what you get from a certain action minus what you give up for it. In the usual monetary system of understanding, the modern accounting sense, profit is typically understood as the amount of revenue earned from selling goods and services minus the monetary costs incurred to produce and sell the items.

As many people know, we usually have to give up a great deal of nonmonetary things in order to secure a high monetary profit or wage. The additional cost is sometimes in terms of time away from home, family relationships compromised, missed trips to Disney World, or years of non-productivity and effort in advanced education.

We are conditioned in modern times to think of profit only in terms of money. That, again, is the narrow view. In the accounting sense, it is necessary to use monetary measures, because that is the primary objective way we have to view external results. In a deeper sense, however, we profit any time that we feel we are better off after our chosen action than we were before.

---

[8] Modern King James Version. The NIV doesn't use the word "profit," but this is the sense of profit that is applicable to our discussion.

At the grocery store, do I get the item that is cheaper or do I pay more for something that I will enjoy more, something that gives me more satisfaction overall or lasts longer? With this set of alternatives, it may be weighing the monetary cost against a nonmonetary characteristic. Even the monetary costs, however, have to do with comparing, on some level, consciously or unconsciously, the things we have to do without if we pay this money. When Jesus spoke of cost, the point he made was that there is a real cost of following him. The other side of the coin is that there is a real cost of not following him, and each person who considers it chooses that which he or she considers more profitable.

People have their own reasons for valuing various goods. There is a market even for very high-priced flowers or expensive, exotic fruits and vegetables. The high price doesn't mean that they can't compete with lower-cost goods, as long as people perceive that they get value for the money spent. The key to a monetary profit is to compete in a market where the price of the good, as determined by the market, is higher than the costs to produce it.

How can an entrepreneur be sure that the market that he or she enters will be profitable? He or she can't. Competition has been described as an ongoing, "rivalrous" discovery process. The market system is dynamic, always adjusting to changes in the environment. That environment includes everything that can possibly affect supply and demand for any product. Because conditions are constantly changing, there is no guarantee that the market conditions for any product will prevail for any length of time. Those who make a profit merely demonstrate that they have discovered a process that works, at least for today, from among the nearly infinite variety of possible processes. Those people who incur a loss demonstrate that they have found a process that doesn't work. The goal of the ongoing discovery process is to find another way that works better and more efficiently.

As economic conditions change, there may be less room in a

particular market for competitors. Profitable processes may become unprofitable. The least efficient producers may be forced out of business. That is not good for the competitor who may lose money or even go bankrupt. That person or those people may have to find new jobs or new careers. The change may be painful.

The change due to competition is, however, very good for society, as a whole. As producers become more efficient, real prices decrease, as does the real cost of living. Fewer hours of work are needed to supply the basic needs of a family and of the whole society. More hours are left over for producing additional value for the family, for recreation or charity, or anything else that is important to the individual.

People who leave one market or occupation are not destined to be unemployed forever, however. Increased productivity frees up resources to be used in other endeavors as the economy spirals upward. A dramatic example from history will illustrate how this works.

In early America, as in all countries before the industrial age, a very large percentage of the population was employed in agriculture. Today, approximately 2% of the population provides food for all the rest of us and for export. That doesn't mean that 98% of the population has become unemployed because they don't work in agriculture. It means that agriculture has become so efficient that most people would be better off using their skills in other occupations. They are able to add much more value and earn a higher profit from their efforts by building cars or teaching students, whether that profit is measured in the wages an employer pays for the services, the revenue earned from customers for goods and services provided, or other nonmonetary forms of profit.

The economy continually evolves. New industries emerge and others fade. Many of the jobs held by the workers of today didn't even exist twenty years ago. New industries are typically more efficient than others they replace, but not nearly as efficient as the ones into which they will evolve. As time goes on, the new industries will become old industries. The higher capital investment and the resulting high productivity of the employees will mean that fewer employees will be needed. The next turn of the wheel will open up new opportunities for those who can no longer compete where they may have, at one time, been very profitable.

This cycle highlights another very important function that profits serve in a market economy. As an industry matures, more competitors become very efficient, and real (inflation adjusted) prices decline. This makes it more difficult for some producers to remain profitable.

When those competitors leave the market, where do the resources that are freed up go? They will tend to migrate toward those areas of the economy that need them most. People will go where it is easiest to be profitable and easiest to get a job. Materials not used in the old industry will tend to be used in more profitable ventures and transfer to areas where they are needed.

The reason that a particular market is highly profitable is that the supply is not keeping up with the demand for the good or service. The value created, and thus the price, is high relative to the associated costs. With economic freedom, there is a significant incentive for suppliers to enter the profitable market and those already existing to produce more. That increase in the supply tends to reduce the price over time.

In this way, the price mechanism of free markets is an automatic circuit breaker for high prices. High prices and profits will tend to decrease relatively efficiently where markets are free to adjust. This function of the markets is especially important in the case of severe shortages and gluts, as we will see in section 3.

15. Trade and Capital

Trade and capital accumulation foster economic progress.

A wife of noble character who can find? ... She is like merchant ships, bringing food from afar... She considers a field and buys it; out of her earnings she plants a vineyard. She sets about her work vigorously; her arms are strong for the tasks. She sees that her trading is profitable... (Prv 31:10, 14, 16–18)

One of the key benefits of an awareness of true economic principles is the ability to understand progress in societies over time. It is readily apparent that every region around the globe with a developed economy has progressed from primitive tribes to prosperous centers of trade at varying rates, and the present circumstances of those regions are dramatically different.

Why are some societies advancing in the Information Age, while others have not advanced beyond a primitive existence? Leaving the presumption of the goodness or badness of progress aside,[9] the fundamental concepts discussed previously can explain the reality of the differences. It often helps to have a visual model to bring concepts together for greater understanding, such as we have

---

[9] Some people see economic progress as inherently bad and try to block it as much as possible. That discussion is beyond the scope of this book, but the view taken here is that progress is, most definitely and demonstrably, good for everyone involved. It is the right of people in each society, however, to decide whether they want to do what is required by progress. Some people are happy without development. They must, however, also accept a lower standard of living that accompanies the shunning of development.

seen with the relationship between supply and demand.

Mainstream economists typically look at the economic system as a circular flow, with households on one side and businesses on the other side. The households provide the labor and other factors needed by businesses for production. The businesses produce the goods that, in turn, are supplied to and purchased by the households. The flow of money is in the opposite direction.

The optimal condition in this view of the system is equilibrium, where all parts of the system are in perfect balance. While there is some usefulness in that conception, the circular-flow equilibrium is static and is less than satisfying when looking at the real world and progress in societies over time. An economy in perfect balance can never improve.

Using the concepts introduced previously, we can build a visual model of economic reality that helps us to understand why some societies progress and others stagnate or decline. The model for development assumes that resources, meaning matter and energy in their various forms, are useless to the satisfaction of human wants and needs until they are changed, by some definite, chosen transformation process, to a form and/or location that will make them more usable. This transformation process is commonly called production. It is the application of some form of human labor to increase the value of some resource, which includes the very limited resource of time.

Production is the core of every economic system and is the source of all wealth, prosperity, and progress. It is the engine that drives improvement and development in society. Progress, in the sense used here, is the reduction of effort and time needed for the participants to satisfy their needs and increase their overall well being.

The real test of progress is the absolute condition of the poorest members of society. In advanced societies, the poorest people are generally far better off than a great majority of the population in less developed countries. Development has a correlation with economic freedom. The poor in America and other countries with a high level or economic freedom have an average income nine times higher than that of the poor in the least free, least developed countries.[10]

There is a very understandable reason for this. As a society advances, it takes less time and effort to produce the goods needed. This leads to lower real (inflation adjusted) money prices over time. With low relative money prices, those with limited resources are able to satisfy their needs more easily than with higher prices. The further an economy progresses, the lower the real cost and the easier it is for the poor to live happier, healthier, more comfortable lives.

Figure 4, on the next page, is a visual model of an economic system that shows the mechanism for progress, meaning that less effort and time is required to produce what is needed and desired. It is one way to understand, in simplified terms, the advancement of a society.

At the center of the model lies production, the prosperity machine. Resources of matter and energy are taken into the machine at the top. Human labor of some sort turns the handle, and goods and services come out the bottom. The faster the handle is turned, the more goods and services are produced. A flywheel is a device for using momentum to keep the machine going, and, in the model, the flywheel is made of capital investment.

Notice that the production from the system can go one of two ways, toward consumption or toward investment. While the purpose of production is for the satisfaction of human needs and wants, when a certain amount of the production is diverted to investment, it adds to the mass of the flywheel that helps to turn the handle. The bigger the flywheel is, the more that its momentum helps keep the

---

[10] James D. Gwartney and Robert Lawson, with Seth Norton, *Economic Freedom of the World: 2014 Report*, (Economic Freedom Network, 2014), xxii. Also available at fraserinstitute.org and freetheworld.com.

machine running and the less human effort is needed to maintain it.

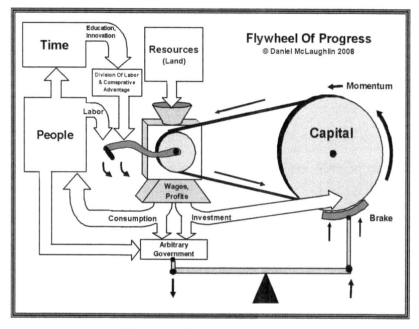

Figure 1-Flywheel of Progress

In primitive societies with little or no capital investment, all production is through the brute force of labor. There is no momentum to help turn the handle. Primitive people engage in difficult physical labor for long hours every day just to survive. Their production is limited to what they can physically do with the simple implements they have.

In contrast, advanced societies have built up large flywheels of capital. As the flywheel spins, it helps to turn the handle. Thus it takes fewer hours per person and less physical labor overall to maintain a certain standard of living.

The division of labor also helps to turn the crank, making it even easier as people become more productive. The time that is saved can be used by individuals for increased leisure activities or for education and skill improvement, which can further enhance the division of labor and its positive effect on productive ability.

International and interregional trade expands the area over which the benefits of division of labor and comparative advantage can be maximized. Once again, the more areas of trade, the bigger the force on the handle running the machine. Expanded trade enables people to live better lives with less effort.

As seen from the diagram, the greater the forces from the momentum of capital, division of labor, and comparative advantage, the less physical labor and the less average time per person is required to produce the goods necessary to sustain or increase a standard of living. The book of Proverbs in the Old Testament referred to the benefits of human-labor-saving assets even in biblical times: "Where there are no oxen, the manger is empty, but from the strength of an ox comes an abundant harvest." (Prv 14:4)

Looking at the economy in this way, it becomes apparent why some societies soar while others flounder. Those societies that have economic freedom, where property rights are honored and people can make their own decisions, have the highest likelihood of progress. It results from the incentives built into the system of free societies. When people are able to profit from their investments in capital and from their efforts at education and efficiency, they have the incentive to do so. They enhance their productive capacity and improve the standard of living.

On the other hand, without solid property rights, there is much less incentive to make any improvements. In that case, any benefit from the efforts may be confiscated. The reduction of property rights can be viewed as arbitrary government siphoning off production. It not only reduces the amount of production available for consumption or investment, but as bureaucracy increases in size, it actually acts as a drag or a brake on the economy, depleting momentum.

Arbitrary government is defined here as the formal or informal use of force to confiscate property or coerce the population. It can be the active taking of property or it can be the prevention of property owners from protecting themselves from predators, those from both within and outside of government.

There is a correlation between economic freedom and reduced poverty. In general, the societies that are the poorest are those where economic freedom is the lowest.[11] Their governments are run by dictators or a democratic tyranny of the majority, which can confiscate property, either directly or through confiscatory taxes. There is heavy bureaucracy and little buildup of capital. People don't invest in expensive labor-saving equipment or facilities because assets, or the value they produce, may be taken from them. Lenders won't lend if it is likely that they won't get their money back. Without lending and profits, it is unlikely that there will be much, if any, entrepreneurship and capital accumulation.

The ancient story of Ali Baba and the forty thieves[12] is enlightening with respect to conditions where property rights are weak or lacking. People of that time and locality had little protection for their property. They recognized that any wealth they accumulated was at a high risk, and, therefore, they tended to bury it in the ground. According to the legend, the forty thieves hid their magnificent plunder in a magic cave. Ali Baba heard the magic words used by the thieves to open the door of the cave. When the thieves had gone, he spoke the words, secretly entered the cave, and took some of the coins.

He, in turn, had to hide the money he took from the cave in a hole in his backyard. He could not use it, because it would arouse jealousy and suspicion among his neighbors, and the thieves might find him out. In that situation, wealth is of very little use to anyone.

---

[11] James Gwartney and Robert Lawson, 27.

[12] "One Thousand and One Nights," a collection of ancient tales from the Middle East.

While the story is only a fable, it was a reflection of the times and the values held by real people. That society has a lot in common with many less-developed countries of today.

Compare that situation to the Dutch golden age of the 17th and 18th centuries. Instead of burying their accumulated wealth in the ground or a cave, they used it to build ocean vessels and other productive assets to use in trade. They built up their capital to make their labors much more productive. Trade was their source of wealth, and the early Dutch cities were centers of progress, prosperity, and culture. Respect for property rights was the foundation for expanded trade.

The rise of the merchant class and widespread trading systems of the European Middle Ages led to the conditions that enabled people to take better advantage of the division of labor and comparative advantage.[13] Major centers of trade became the source of wealth for the region. "Unlike China and the ancient empires, the Europe of the late medieval city-states and the early monarchies came to the age of discovery without a central authority strong enough to check the determination of its merchants to gain access to profitable trading opportunities...."[14]

Those profitable trading opportunities led to the accumulation of wealth in Western countries. They also meant that everyday people were able to satisfy their needs better and more cheaply, thus raising their standard of living. The rise of the West was a phenomenon that wasn't just a coincidence that accompanied the flowering of freedom and markets; it was, rather, the direct result of it. It is a pattern that is vigorously resisted in many parts of the world that are in desperate need of it to emerge from the mire of poverty.

The freedom of merchants to trade was necessarily matched by

---

[13] Nathan Rosenberg and L. E. Birdzell, Jr., *How the West Grew Rich,* (New York, Basic Book Publishers, 1986, p. 77.

[14] Rosenberg and Birdzell, p. 61.

its corollary—individuals trading with merchants, which greatly expanded the market for the goods and services of those individuals to a much wider area and a broader market. It also meant that goods from outside the local area were now available for them to buy, enhancing their standard of living far beyond what it would have been.

Gross Domestic Product (GDP) is a statistical measure that attempts to gauge productivity in a society. While it can be useful, an increase in GDP is not always progress. The statistics necessarily can't take all factors into consideration, and they also may include factors that confuse the issue. What really matters is whether the individuals are better off or not. Aggregate statistics can, and often do, mislead. They can give political impetus to use inappropriate policies that don't promote real long-term growth, but rather causes distortion of economic reality.

Monetary policy is usually seen by politicians as a lever by which they can manipulate GDP growth in the economy. The manipulation of interest rates and money production, however, only results in what is commonly known as the business cycle, but is more appropriately viewed as a monetary cycle. The rapid expansion and the inevitable contraction of the money supply, greatly amplified by fractional reserve banking, leads to boom periods, followed by devastating bust periods. (See pages 179 to 183, Money and Inflation, for further discussion.)

The overall effect of inflationary expansion on the economy is not real, long-term growth, but serious periodic dislocation. The only real source of long-term growth comes from people investing to make labor more productive and valuable. That investing, in the long run, can only come from savings and wealth accumulation. Investing based on monetary expansion merely redistributes the capital from the general populace to those who create the artificial money, and that makes it more difficult for entrepreneurs to react to true demand from consumers.

Progress comes about from individual capital accumulation, and capital accumulation arises through trade, enabled by division of labor and comparative advantage. Trade can only have its benefits when people have something with which to trade, and the incentive to make it pay off.

Property rights enable people to accumulate some level of wealth over time. Contrary to what many think, wealth, in and of itself, is neither good nor bad. Everyone has different ideas about what things are important to him or her. For some, extra leisure time means they can spend another evening bowling with their friends. Another person might take a second job instead, because he or she has certain goals in mind that require additional financial resources.

In voluntary exchange, it is always true that both parties believe that they will be better off, in some way, after the trade than they were before. If that was not the case, the exchange would not have been made. The future is uncertain, however, and things don't always work out as planned. Thus, people don't always profit from their trades as expected. Those who align their expectations with reality are more likely to make the better decisions and profit the most from their interactions with other people.

When arbitrary decisions are made by ruling authorities that distort the normal economic relationships, it becomes much more difficult for people to know what results to expect from their decisions and efforts. The more distorted the economic environment, the more likely it will be that more people will make the wrong decisions.

The visual model, the Flywheel of Progress, presents a dynamic view of an economy. It recognizes the constantly changing nature of the world. It emphasizes what it takes for progress in the well-being of the individuals living in it. Again, it is merely a simplified, abstract view of the way an economy operates. No model can fully describe reality, and every model has weaknesses. It is, however, an alternative view of economic systems that can help to understand how the complexities of billions of daily inputs can contribute to progress or to decline in a society.

Chapter 31, verses 10–31 of the Book of Proverbs is as concise a summation of the model of economic progress as is written anywhere. It describes the qualities of a wife of noble character, but those noble characteristics apply to all. Those qualities determine the progress of an individual, a family, a country, and the world. It is so powerful and full of truth that it is reproduced in full.

Proverbs 31:10–31

A wife of noble character who can find?
　　She is worth far more than rubies.
Her husband has full confidence in her
　　and lacks nothing of value.
She brings him good, not harm,
　　all the days of her life.
She selects wool and flax
　　and she works with eager hands.
She is like the merchant ships,
　　bringing her food from afar.
She gets up while it is still dark;
　　she provides food for her family
　　and portions for her servant girls.
She considers a field and buys it;
　　out of her earnings she plants a vineyard.
She sets about her work vigorously;
Her arms are strong for the tasks.
She sees that her trading is profitable,
　　And her lamp does not go out at night.
In her hand she holds the distaff
　　And grasps the spindle with her fingers.
She opens her arms to the poor
　　and extends her hands to the needy.

When it snows, she has no fear for her household;
    For all of them are clothed in scarlet.
She makes coverings for her bed;
She is clothed in fine linen and purple.
Her husband is respected at the city gate,
    where he takes his seat among the elders
    of the land.
She makes linen garments and sells them,
    and supplies the merchants with sashes.
She is clothed with strength and dignity;
    she can laugh at the days to come.
She speaks with wisdom,
    And faithful teaching is on her tongue.
She watches over the affairs of her household
    and does not eat the bread of idleness.
Her children arise and call her blessed;
Her husband also, and he praises her:
    "Many women do noble things,
    but you surpass them all."
Charm is deceptive, and beauty fleeting;
    but a woman who fears the Lord is to be praised.
Give her the reward she has earned,
    and let her works bring her praise at the city gate.

16. Resources

Resources come from the human mind.

By the sweat of your brow you will eat your food until you return to the ground, since from it you were taken; for dust you are and to dust you will return. (Gn 3:19)

God created the universe. We reside here on earth, a huge ball of stuff, moving in space. Earth is pretty much a closed system for everything except energy. Meteors may bring substances from space, and we may lose an infinitesimally small portion when space craft leave our atmosphere. Other than that, what we have now is probably pretty much the same as it has always been, though likely in different combinations of the elements. Everything comes from the earth and everything returns to the earth, as the well-known verse from Genesis 3:19 reminds us.

The Earth is a mass of hot, molten substances. The crust has cooled enough for living creatures to survive, but that crust itself traps energy within. The sun drenches the planet with intense, life-giving energy every day. The earth's crust is made of elements, chemical compounds, and mixtures that provide what are often referred to as natural resources. In the most general sense, resources are nothing more than matter and energy combined in different forms.

Resources are typically thought of as limited, and the concept of scarcity is vitally important to all of economics. Opportunity cost, which we have explored earlier, flows from the recognition of the scarcity of the things we desire. There is a limited availability of particular materials, and choices must be made as to how best to satisfy needs with limited supplies of goods.

That is very true in the short term. It is not so evident on a long-term time scale, however. It may seem counterintuitive, but, in a very real sense, the resources available to satisfy human needs are virtually unlimited. It is the vast abundance of God's promise.

In his groundbreaking work, Julian Lincoln Simon (1932–1998) demonstrated that, for all practical purposes relevant to human life and progress, resources are infinite. How can this be? Engineers can approximate the content of the earth, the quantity of various substances, the volume of oceans, and so on. The amount they calculate is obviously a finite quantity. Given that reality, it would seem that resources would have a definite limit and that using up any quantity would make it unavailable for the future.

The ultimate resource, in Simon's view,[15] is the human mind. As people live their lives, they encounter problems. The human mind is endowed with the ability to analyze the situation and to come up with a way around the problem. People use the things that are available to them to improve their lives. This is true, not only today, but also true of biblical times, and, indeed, the earliest human civilizations.

It is not a coincidence that modern developed countries with large-scale economic freedom and trade have never had a devastating famine. The world has never run out of any type of resource, and it is unlikely that it ever will, as long as there are free people willing and able to use their God-given intelligence. There will always be matter and energy in its various forms, and production is merely the transformation of matter and energy from one form into a form more suitable to solve the problems encountered in life and progress. In order to understand why this is so, we can use the concepts we have developed so far.

---

[15] Julian L. Simon, *The Ultimate Resource* Princeton, New Jersey: Princeton University Press, 1981, revised edition, 1996), 589.

Cost, as we have seen, involves what we have to give up so we can get what we want. If something costs more, it is only so because it uses resources that people consider more dear. Input costs do not determine the price, but rather the relationship between supply and demand does. Costs do, however, determine the minimum profitable price and, therefore, the lower limit toward which prices tend to fall in free markets over an extended period of time. A cheaper price will generally mean that real resources of a lower relative value are used.

We have all heard the remark about saving a tree by not using paper. However true that may be, paper is cheap because pulp wood is a very available and renewable resource. It is farmed and managed much like any other crop. The tree that you save by not using paper will be offset by something else of more value if the substitute is more expensive than paper.

By saving a tree, you may be wasting time or many other resources that could have been used for something much more productive and valuable. Of course, it is never a good idea to waste anything, but conservation itself is a tradeoff between various opportunity costs.

The current energy situation is another good case to consider. Petroleum is a resource that takes a long time and a great deal of investment to develop. When prices are high, there is an incentive to invest more in discovery and extraction. The high prices give more profits, which enable and give incentive for even more exploration and development.

It also gives incentive for new competitors to enter the market to develop more supply. That development, once in place, will affect the supplies both for the present and for a long time into the future. That increased supply will force prices down and will maintain downward pressure for years.

The inverse happens on the demand side. High petroleum prices cause the development of more efficient manufacturing facilities, equipment, homes, and motor vehicles, in fact, of all of the uses for petroleum products. The high prices also reduce the quantity demanded at present. They encourage the development of alternative forms of energy and more efficient processes. Those increased efficiencies are long term and are still available when the petroleum prices decline.

When the permanent productivity gains of suppliers and efficiency gains of demanders are combined, it creates the tendency for the long-term decline in the price of energy in real terms. That is, in reality, the long-term tendency from the time when the cave man first harnessed fire.

If and when real deposits of petroleum start to dwindle permanently, the price of petroleum-based products in a free market will increase permanently, encouraging the alternatives and discouraging the use of petroleum. Petroleum will become very economically inefficient and its use will decline. We will never run out because it will get too expensive and create profitable opportunities for alternatives long before the point of running dry. It is not anything that government policy can or should be involved in. It will happen naturally in free markets, because the market provides the right incentives to adjust behavior to the present reality.

In the 1800s, there was a fear that the rise of industry and production would falter because the supply of coal, the primary energy source at the time, would be depleted.[16] There are today, however, vastly greater quantities of known coal reserves than in the 1800s, even though the use of coal has increased dramatically as time progressed. The same goes for petroleum, natural gas, and virtually every other source of energy. That may not always be the

---

[16] William Stanley Jevons (1835–1882), *The Coal Question: An Enquiry Concerning the Progress of the Nation and the Probable Exhaustion of Our Coal-Mines,* (London: Macmillan, 1865; 2nd revised edition, 1866; 3rd revised edition, 1906; reprint, New York: A. M. Kelley, 1965), 3.

case. Limited supplies of a particular resource, however, are not cause for despair.

If it gets to the point that higher prices are not able to wring more petroleum from the ground, then, given that markets are free to react, the short supply will push prices ever higher, to the point that alternative forms of energy will become profitable on their own. The new profits in those energy forms will encourage their development, and the cycle will go on as it has since the beginning of civilization. The price of petroleum will then drop again as demand drops, and it will still be available for the processes for which it is best suited. If you consider all of the various forms of energy in God's abundant creation, it is not even conceivable that human society will ever run out of energy, as long as that society consists of markets where people are free to innovate and to profit from developing the always abundant alternatives.

The same analysis can be done for any resource. There has never been an episode in history where there has been a complete depletion of even one single mineral resource. That is pretty amazing, when you consider the implications.

What happens when a scarce resource is consumed, say platinum used in catalytic converters of automobiles? The car is worn out eventually, and it may take a one-way trip to the junk yard. Does that mean that the platinum ceases to be platinum? Does that mean that, once the car is junked, its reuse is forever removed as a possibility available for human society? Obviously not.

The metal and other materials in the junk yard are still available for current or future generations to discover and use in any way that is useful for them. When the cost of mining iron increases, the re-use of steel from junked cars becomes more cost effective. We have seen various episodes when junk yards were emptied of formerly worthless scrap heaps. If junk cars sit around for years in a junk yard, that is only because it is more efficient to use fresh iron mined from the ground. The incentives of the market automatically direct the resources to the most efficient use.

Even the paper from that tree that was cut down is not lost when it is consumed. It will likely end up in a landfill somewhere, along with millions of tons of other metals, plastics, papers, etc. While that may be a significant problem in the relatively short term, the matter and energy that are stored there never go away. It has merely returned to the dust, as Genesis 3:19 profoundly states about human beings. Sometime in the future, those landfills may offer an efficient source of materials. Production processes would again transform the matter and energy into different combinations to solve the problems of that time efficiently.

In short, there is every reason to be optimistic about the future of human society and its ability to adjust to changing conditions and resource availability, given that people and markets are free to use their creative intelligence and God's vast abundance.

17. Good Intentions

Good intentions don't equal good results.

Can a man scoop fire into his lap without his clothes being burned? Can a man walk on hot coals without his feet being scorched? (Prv 6:27–28)

"The road to hell is paved with good intentions." That is an old familiar proverb that is not biblical, but rings true to most of us. A biblical equivalent to it appears twice in different places with identical wording, which serves to give it more emphasis: "There is a way that seems right to a man, but in the end it leads to death." (Prv 14:12 and 16:25)

The idea behind both versions is that good intentions don't matter if you ignore reality and don't do what is necessary to achieve those intentions. If you need to get to the bottom of a cliff quickly to help someone who is injured, that good intention is not going to matter if you step off the edge and disregard gravity. Your death or injury will be just as certain as if you were trying to kill yourself.

The proverbs, and the entire Bible for that matter, are filled with admonishments to the wise and to the foolish. Get wisdom, avoid foolishness. Wisdom includes knowing not just the commandments, but also the laws of God's ordered world. The wise live according to the physical and the economic laws that provide the order and regularity on which we rely. The foolish ignore the laws and suffer the consequences.

We find a lot of foolishness in our world. The way that appears right may "lead to death," as the proverbs state it, because that way is relying on fallacies or looking only at half truths. It is not taking all of the truth into consideration.

Forty Centuries of Wage and Price Controls,[17] by Robert Schuettinger and Eamonn Butler, outlines a series of interventions and controls imposed by various governments over four millennia. The disastrous effects of bureaucracy and interventionism were the same for the ancient Sumerians and Babylonians as they are for governments today. People have not learned from history, and many millions more people will suffer and die needless, premature deaths in the future as they are sacrificed on the altars of the false gods of government saviors.

The Broken-Window Fallacy

In the mid 1800s, a French economist, Frédéric Bastiat (1801–1850), used a type of parable, short stories with lessons, to help people understand economic principles. They hold just as true for us today. He wrote about the consequences of half truths and illustrated what we now know as "the broken-window fallacy."[18] He described the case of a shopkeeper whose window had been broken by his careless son. Onlookers told him that, while it was unfortunate for the shop keeper, breaking glass is good because it keeps the glazier in business. The money paid to the glazier supports his employees and suppliers, and that, in turn, is good for trade and industry as a whole, as that money ripples ever outward into the economy.

That describes only the half that is seen. Everyone knows that

---

[17] Schuettinger and Butler, *Forty Centuries of Wage and Price Controls: How Not to Fight Inflation,* by Robert Lindsay Schuettinger (born 1936) and Eamon F. Butler (Washington, D.C.: Heritage Foundation; Thornwood, New York: distributed by Caroline House, 1979).

[18] Frédéric Bastiat, "What Is Seen and Unseen," 1850 essay, reprinted in *The Libertarian Reader* (New York: The Free Press, 1997), 265.

the glazier benefits, along with his employees and suppliers and everyone with whom they may trade in turn. They can see that part. The other half is what is unseen. It takes a keener sense to recognize that there is more to the story than meets the eye. Because the shopkeeper paid the money to the glazier, he no longer has that money available to buy shoes or books or anything else he might want to buy.

The money that benefits the glazier will now not support the cobbler or bookseller. They will not be able to pay their employees and suppliers, and that loss also ripples out to the rest of the economy. The best that can come of it is that the trade gained and the trade lost even out. There can be no net benefit to total industry by the destruction of the window. The destruction of the window has reduced the wealth of the shopkeeper, and in so doing, has reduced the wealth of society.

Destruction can never make the victims or society better off. It can only decrease wealth. Wars, hurricanes, and arson only make it necessary to produce more to get back to where you started, much the same as in the case of the foolish man who built his house upon the sand in Jesus' parable. Some people may be made better off, but that only occurs because others are worse off.

Even in the case of what is called "creative destruction," the replacement of old productive assets with newer, more productive technology, it is not the destruction that is bringing the benefit, but only the new technology. It is a rational decision to purchase the new technology because it is recognized that, in doing so, the investment will pay more than the old technology and add more wealth than is lost in the outdated assets. It is the anticipation of net benefits, which fits with every other economic concept discussed so far.

You will find, without looking very hard, examples of the broken-window fallacy popping up in everyday conversation and in the speeches of seemingly wise politicians. Even highly trained but very careless economists often fall victim. If you look below the surface, you will find a special interest acting as the glazier, looking for a benefit, using arguments that the taking of money from someone else and giving it to him or her will spur trade and industry or "stimulate" the economy. You will find politicians as mischievous window breakers, helping the glazier and getting rewarded with votes, campaign contributions, or some other form of bribery. You may also find a crowd of people cheering on the destruction, not able to look below the surface to see the error of ignoring the unseen.

Moral Hazard

Moral hazard occurs when people are insulated from the risks and consequences of their actions, while retaining or accumulating the benefits. Moral hazard tends to skew people's choices to the detriment of others. There are many examples that result from the myriad of government programs, but one will be sufficient to give the idea.

There is a relatively high risk in locating your home or business on a flood plain. It can be predicted fairly accurately that there will be extensive damage on a repeating basis. Insuring property on a flood plain is very expensive, in recognition of the very high risks involved. Under normal circumstances, this would discourage people from building in such a risky area. They would be subject to too much exposure to loss. They would have to use their valuable resources to keep rebuilding instead of using it to improve their lives or to invest in their future.

Normal insurance policies anticipate the full costs of damages and charge a premium in proportion to the risk of loss. If a particular area gets hit with a devastating flood every ten years on average, it means that the annual average cost of flood damage would be one tenth of the actual average damage from the flooding, with additional charges for insurance administration. For a house with $100,000 damage on average, a normal insurance policy would need to collect premiums of more than ten thousand dollars per year to cover that one house. The high annual cost would discourage most people from building there. The situation is magnified for multimillion-dollar mansions built in dangerous locations.

If, on the other hand, cheap, taxpayer-funded flood insurance and federal disaster assistance assures that the losses will be incurred by taxpayers instead of the owners, people are then encouraged to build in high-risk locations. As a result, over time, more damage is done, more lives are put at risk, and taxpayers have a spiraling cost for covering the damage that should never have happened. Taxpayer-funded flood insurance and disaster assistance has the perverse effect of increasing the damage and loss of life from floods and hurricanes. The removal of responsibility from the individuals makes the individuals irresponsible.

Incentives Affect Decisions

People act because they expect to be better off. That is generally the way the economy works, whether or not the people are free. Under conditions of free markets, the incentives balance the needs of everyone and, because trade and transactions are strictly voluntary, conflict is minimized.

Under conditions where people are not free, such as those in the former Soviet Union, they still make decisions on the same basis as everyone else. The only thing that changes is that the range of choices is restricted. Instead of being allowed to enter into any voluntary arrangement that does not infringe on the rights of others, the people have to choose from less beneficial options determined by a bureaucrat. The restrictions can come in the form of direct commands, as in "you must buy your food at the state store," or merely outlawing one or more of the otherwise available options.

The choices also necessarily factor in the risk of getting caught doing something that the oppressive government prohibits.

When interest rates are held artificially low, the incentive to save is diminished and people have a tendency to save less. There is a tendency in that situation for politicians to use rhetoric or to take actions intended to increase savings. They will be ineffective or lead to other undesirable consequences because the original disincentive is still in place.

When alcoholic beverages or particular drugs are outlawed, there is an incentive to use illegal and dangerous means to get them. In every case, the outlawing of any product that is desired by people can only lead to black markets. Because black markets are outside the law, they give rise to violent criminal gangs, who profit from the increase in prices inevitable with making goods illegal. People die of poisoning from bathtub gin or underground meth-lab drugs. The history of banned products is a history of high prices, black markets, broken lives, and violent crime.

While God calls us to care for our bodies, he does not call us to make civil laws that restrict others from making their own decisions. The freedom to which we are called is also the freedom to which every other individual is called. That freedom, however, requires personal responsibility for the results of our actions.

Protectionism

Protectionism is an old tool used by politicians for many centuries. It is a prime example of the broken-window fallacy, looking only at the short-term immediate effects on one group, rather than the long-term and short-term effects on all groups of people. It is a mechanism by which special interests can extract benefits for themselves from the rest of the population, and it comes in many forms. Import quotas, tariffs, price supports, subsidies, and exclusionary laws keep the price of and profits from specific domestic goods high while increasing the cost of products to the buying public.

The net result in the short run is that the cost of the protected products goes up, leaving the consumer worse off because of higher prices. The high price affects both the wealthy and the poor, but especially hurts the poor. It is, in effect, taking money from the pockets of consumers and putting it into the pockets of the members of the protected industry. The money that goes toward the favored individuals is no longer available for other purchases and non-protected industries, and those industries suffer lower prices and pressure on profits.

Another perverse but neglected result of protectionism is that manufacturers of other goods that depend on the protected products have higher costs and cannot compete with foreign producers. The steel industry in the United States is a good case-in-point, since it is often the beneficiary of significant government protection. Steel is a major component of many products, and a significant component of the production of nearly all products. Legal protections against competition enable the domestic steel manufacturers to maintain high prices. This helps the steel manufactures and everyone connected with them.

The users of steel, on the other hand, are the ones who have to pay for the higher profits of steel producers. Since foreign steel is excluded from the market or made expensive by tariffs, high-priced steel must be used to manufacture cars and trucks, to build bridges and buildings, to form steel pipe, and to make computer components. Each producer of those items has competition from foreign suppliers who aren't subject to the high prices of American steel.

While inefficient American steel factories may stay open and their employees keep their jobs, industries made uncompetitive by high-priced steel have a more difficult time keeping factories open and workers employed. Domestic automobile manufacturers stand out as a shining example. The benefits to the protected industry come involuntarily from the pockets of everyone outside that industry, including the poor, the aged, those on fixed incomes, and everyone else that Christians strive to care for.

In voluntary trade, the parties benefit in proportion to the value they provide. With protectionism, at least some of the benefit to one party comes from coercion rather than providing value. The enforced reduction in trade resulting from protectionism is a drag on the economy and reduces all of the benefits that derive from expanded division of labor and comparative advantage. The net result is that, in the long run, it stifles the economy and impedes progress in the standard of living. With the exception of the protected few, the economy and everyone in it is worse off.

Monopolies/Cartels

Monopoly is the domination of a market by a single seller. A cartel is the collusion of several sellers to control the market. The assumption is that a monopolist or cartel can manipulate the price of the good or service produced by restricting output. As the supply goes down, the price will go up. For some types of goods, the demand declines at a slower rate than the price increases, meaning the monopolist can earn more profit on fewer goods sold. The higher price can be good for the monopolist or cartel, but it is bad for everyone else. Thus, there is an impetus for people to call on government to prevent monopolies and cartels.

The belief that monopolists in a free market can and do restrict output and raise prices does not match the historical record, however according to Professor Thomas DiLorenzo: "Those industries targeted as 'monopolies' grew at seven times the rate of the economy as a whole. In the same period, prices charged by the trusts also fell faster than the general price level did."[19]

Law professor Dominick T. Armentano has written extensively on antitrust and is highly critical of antitrust legislation. He says: "Abusive monopoly is always to be associated with governmental interference in production or exchange, and such situations do injure consumers, exclude sellers, and result in an inefficient misallocation of resources. But importantly for this discussion, such monopoly situations are legal, created and sanctioned by political authority for its own purposes."[20]

Whether or not private monopolies do exist over a long time or hurt consumers, it seems that most people believe that monopolies are bad and should be prevented. That does not prevent people from proposing government monopolies as the solution to all sorts of social ills. It is illogical, however, to say that business owners will abuse power with monopolies, but a government bureaucrat will not abuse even greater power that arises from the compulsion of government. The areas of society that have the most severe problems are those where government has assumed the dominant position in the provision of services. Those organizations that enjoy monopoly power do so because they are sanctioned or explicitly formed by government. They use the coercive power of government to manipulate markets and take money unjustly from the consumers, including the poor. From a practical perspective, the monopoly or near monopoly power of these organizations does not produce good results. Instead, it wreaks havoc in all areas they touch.

Monopoly power is not good in anybody's hands, but it is especially bad in the hands of those who do not have the customer to keep them in line, but rather have a gun to enforce their monopoly.

---

[19] Thomas J. DiLorenzo, *How Capitalism Saved America,* (New York: Three Rivers Press, 2004), 140–141.

[20] Dominick T. Armentano, *Antitrust and Monopoly: Anatomy of a Policy Failure,* (Oakland: The Independent Institute, 1999), 3.

When Good Intentions Work

Good intentions work when they are combined with right principles that reflect the way that the world really works. God calls all Christians to do what is right and good, but he also gave us a framework for knowing what is right and good. That framework is embodied in the Commandments. He gave us an ordered world and human societies that behave in accordance with certain immutable laws, based on physical properties and on the logic of human interaction.

If the good intentions combine with a respect for the commandments, the rights of others, and the physical and economic laws that regulate the world, the results can be very beneficial. If the good intentions go contrary to the laws and ignore the wisdom of the Commandments and the gospel, the results will certainly not be what were expected. More likely, the result will be to make the original problem worse or to introduce new problems to compound those that the good intentions originally attempted to resolve.

Recalling the parable of the two sons referred to in the introduction, saying good and noble words is not the same as doing the things that bring about good and noble results. The results come not from good intentions, but from adhering to the truth established in the Commandments and the laws of God's ordered world.

Part 2

A Common Understanding

18. Agreement on Terms

By wisdom a house is built, and through understanding it is established; through knowledge its rooms are filled with rare and beautiful treasures. (Prv 24:3–4)

It is difficult to have an understanding when the terms used have different meanings for different people. In order to agree, or even to disagree rationally, it is necessary to come to a common understanding of the words used in the discussion.

There is a tendency for the meaning of words to migrate over time. There is also a modern tendency for words to be co-opted by various groups to use the powerful images embodied in them to support a cause counter to the original meaning. This creates a great deal of confusion in dealing with the issues of the day, because people can talk different languages while using the same words.

Part 2 is an attempt to establish a common understanding of several important terms and concepts that have significant implications in discussions of economics and moral or political issues. While the following discussions are not the only way to interpret the terms, they are interpretations undergirded by the author's understanding of the Bible. Whether or not anyone agrees with the interpretations, it is necessary to state them clearly to prevent misunderstandings and to have a meaningful and productive discussion of the issues in part 3.

19. Ethics and Morality

Anyone who breaks one of the least of these commandments and teaches others to do the same will be called least in the kingdom of heaven, but whoever practices and teaches these commands will be called great in the kingdom of heaven. (Mt 5:19)

True economic principles tell us what is. They describe reality and show us the way things work. They lay bare the cause-and-effect relationships in society and human interaction. They are not able to tell us what should be. They are not able to tell us what is good or what is bad. To the extent that an economist, or any scientist, for that matter, tells us what is good or bad or what should be, he or she has taken off the objective economist's or scientist's hat and put on the hat of the ordinary citizen of the human race, whose views are subjective and not provably correct or incorrect.

He or she is no more qualified to say what is good or bad than you or I or anyone else. His or her economic expertise or scientific knowledge is only valuable for describing reality, much the same as that of a chemist. That description can be either accurate or inaccurate. Assuming that the picture of reality is accurate, each decision maker must judge what he or she should do about that reality, given the uncertainty of future events.

Views about what is good and bad are subject to a person's assumptions about reality. Those assumptions may arise from a variety of circumstances, including family childhood experiences, reading and education, work and social experiences, and religious background. Most religions have some kind of written scripture that helps to define good and bad. The Christian religion relies on the Bible as the primary reliable source of guidance for what is good and bad. The keys to all of the teachings of Jesus are the Ten Commandments and the Golden Rule, or the Law of Love, which appear at the front of this book.

The most fundamental principles in the Christian gospel are the recognition and love of God, respect for other people, and appreciation of their rights. "You shall not steal" is recognition that people own property. If it was acquired without stealing, nobody else has the right to take it away from the owner. "You shall not murder" is recognition that people own their own bodies and lives. Nobody has the right to use violence against them.

All of the commandments point toward a way of living that will result in minimal conflict. Respect for the rights of other human beings will reduce the likelihood of conflict arising. Of course, there will always be conflict in the world, because people often ignore the commandments. They covet, they steal, they injure, they murder, they conspire to subvert the will of God for their own benefit.

In all cases, ongoing conflict in the world is due to breaking the commandments. Many people do not have the benefit of knowing them, and thus, it is at least more understandable that they may not respect other people. Christians have no excuse. The Apostle Paul said, "God does not show favoritism. All who sin apart from the law will also perish apart from the law, and all who sin under the law will be judged by the law" (Rom 2:11–12), the law meaning God's law, as embodied in the Ten Commandments.

We, as Christians, are bound by the Commandments. We shall not steal, nor have people steal for us. We shall not injure other people, nor have others do the injury for us. We shall not covet what other people have. God made an abundant world, and he created people to be free. That freedom carries responsibilities. It doesn't carry any guarantees. We are expected to trust Him.

The gospel of Jesus tells us what is good and bad. The laws of mankind are not good unless they reflect God's law. Jesus said of the laws of the Pharisees: "These people honor me with their lips, but their hearts are far from me. They worship me in vain; their teachings are but rules taught by men." (Mt 15:8–9)

In all our dealings in daily life, the law that is most important is the law of love taught by Jesus: "'Love the Lord your God with all your heart and with all your soul and with all your mind.' This is the first and greatest commandment. And the second is like it: 'Love your neighbor as yourself.'" (Mt 22:37–39)

If you love your neighbors, you will help them in their need, you will be generous and kind. You will not covet or steal what is theirs, or cheat or murder or injure. You will not lie. You will honor and care for your family. If you love your God, you will honor him with everything you do, thank him for the wonderful creation and the beauty and abundance in it. You will keep his commandments.

Christians need to worry less about determining what is good and bad. They already have a pretty good roadmap. They do, however, need to be concerned about following the roadmap. There is a tendency for modern Christians to develop a complex rationale to justify breaking the commandments and creating their own system of ethics, deciding on what is good and bad apart from God's law. It is the same error for which Jesus chastised the Pharisees, Sadducees, and other teachers of the law.

Ethics for Christians can only be understood as they relate to the law revealed in the gospel. The Ten Commandments provide the foundation for all rights, which requires respect for the lives of other people and everything they rightfully own.

20. Wealth and Poverty

Command those who are rich in this present world not to be arrogant nor to put their hope in wealth, which is so uncertain, but to put their hope in God, who richly provides us with everything for our enjoyment. Command them to do good, to be rich in good deeds, and to be generous and willing to share. In this way, they will lay up treasure for themselves as a firm foundation for the coming age, so that they may take hold of the life that is truly life (1 Tm 6:17–19)

Wealth is a key aspect in understanding the progress of societies out of destitution toward a state of being where there are fewer poor, and where the poor are better fed, clothed, and housed. It is also a significant stumbling block, because some people see all wealth as evil. Since there is a wide variation in the understanding of the concept of wealth, it is necessary first to settle on a definition in order to have a cohesive discussion.

For our purposes, we will define wealth as a measurement of the level of accumulation of things needed or desired by people. Thus, everyone has a certain degree of wealth, from the poorest to the richest. Riches arc an abundance of wealth, poverty is a scarcity of wealth.

Wealth is the product of human effort, ingenuity, and cooperation. Wealth provides food, shelter, and clothing for the rich and the poor, and no wealth occurs without human activities. Even the baking of bread is the creation of a certain amount of wealth and requires the growing and processing of wheat or other grains into a form that is more usable for human consumption. All wealth creation is the conversion of some resource into something of more value. It comes from the production, by people, of the things that satisfy human wants and needs.

In the quotation above from the letter to Timothy, however, Paul tells him that people should put their trust in God rather than in wealth. Wealth is uncertain, because life is full of uncertainty. The point that Paul makes is that, while crops may fail, wars may devastate, buildings may crumble, and economies may crash, God's treasure is certain. We may not like our present circumstances because of things that happen in this uncertain world, but we are still called to be faithful. We are still subject to the commandments, and we still can hope in the God who watches over us.

Paul also offers the encouraging words: ". . . for I have learned to be content whatever the circumstances. I know what it is to be in need, and I know what it is to have plenty. I have learned the secret of being content in any and every situation, whether well fed or hungry, whether living in plenty or in want. I can do everything through him who gives me strength." (Phil 4:11–13)

The gospel of Jesus originated in a time when many people viewed great wealth as a sign of blessedness, and poverty as being out of favor with God. Rich people saw themselves as the righteous ones. They looked down on the poor as sinners and, thus, less worthy. They viewed their wealth as the badge of privilege, as their sign of high status in the eyes of God.

Jesus' message for them was that, because they put their trust in their riches and not in God, "It is easier for a camel to pass through the eye of a needle than for a rich man to enter the kingdom of God." Their pride and pompousness, lack of love and concern for the less fortunate, their following the letter of the law while still cheating, stealing, and injuring showed that they were not worthy of the kingdom.

Does this mean that accumulation of any wealth is necessarily bad, that no rich people can have any hope of heaven, that poverty is a requirement for all Christians? It certainly is not true if you take the whole gospel into account. The quotation from the first letter to

Timothy recognized that rich people can be generous, willing to share, and rich in good deeds. When the disciples asked Jesus, "Who then can be saved?" Jesus' answer was "With man this is impossible, but with God, all things are possible." (Mt 19:25–26) Salvation comes only from God. When the rich person trusts in his wealth, he does not trust in God. The rich people of whom Jesus spoke believed that their wealth was their salvation and seal of approval from God, and their lack of trust and faith separated them from God.

Proverbs and the Psalms speak often of wealth and prosperity: "Honor the Lord with your wealth, with the first fruits of your crops; then your barns will be filled to overflowing." (Ps 3:9–10) "My son, do not forget my teaching, but keep my commandments in your heart, for they will prolong your life many years and bring you prosperity." (Ps 3:1–2) In the second letter of Paul to the Corinthians, he said, "Now he who supplies seed to the sower and bread for food will also supply and increase your store of seed and will enlarge the harvest of your righteousness. You will be made rich in every way so that you can be generous on every occasion, and through us your generosity will result in thanksgiving to God."(2 Cor 9:10–11)

In Paul's words to Timothy, he admonished the rich to be generous and not to put their trust in their riches. He didn't require them to become poverty-stricken. In Jesus' discussion with the rich young man, when asked what he must do to have eternal life, Jesus replied "If you want to enter life [*eternal life*], obey the commandments." (Mt 19:17)[21]

---

[21] When the young man pressed him further, he said "If you want to be perfect, go sell your possessions and give to the poor, and you will have treasure in heaven. Then, come follow me." Jesus' always knew what his listeners needed to hear. The rich man was proud of his riches and his self righteousness. This is not a command for everyone to sell everything that they own, however. Even the apostle Peter had a house and home which

Obeying the commandments is as important as faith. Saying you are faithful is to no avail if you break God's law. When wealth is gotten by theft, violence, or coercion, obviously the commandments were not followed. In this case, the person with the wealth is evil, because the means to attain it were evil.

In section 1, we saw that, in a society of truly voluntary trade, or free markets, profits arise from meeting the needs of others. If a person adjusts his or her activities and processes so that he or she is able to serve the needs of many people, the result will likely lead to more profit and a higher level of wealth. That is a very good thing. That is the prosperity that God promises. That prosperity can lead to great generosity. On the flip side, there are many warnings about ill-gotten gain.

Wealth, when attained by following God's law, is an implement for good. The prosperity of one person is in no way a detriment to any other person, except when it was gotten through force or fraud. Properly acquired wealth is the source of all charity and the source of progress from poverty to prosperity for any society.

Wealth, however, is also a temptation. People can fall away from God because they fall in love with their wealth. As with the rich people in Jesus' time, their pride may separate them from God. They may use their riches for violence, to injure others, and to attain political control. Those people will find the snare that waits for those who abuse their power and wealth.

While devotion of one's life to the seeking of wealth at all costs and at the expense of everyone else is destructive to the individual and to others, the destruction of wealth and the wealthy out of envy will also lead to bitter fruit. Those who have accumulated some amount of wealth are the only source of charity for those who have fallen on hard times. They are also the source of progress for a

---

Jesus visited to heal his mother-in-law (Mt 8: 13–15.) The apostle Matthew also had a house where Jesus ate dinner. (Mt 9: 10).

society in which individuals can use wealth to produce more efficiently, lowering the costs of living to all, including the poor.

It is very encouraging that in free societies, those which cherish and uphold the requirements of the commandments, the standard of living for the poor is significantly higher than that of the average inhabitant of the earth. It is many times higher than that of the poor in unfree countries and those which arbitrarily restrict voluntary trade. That is neither surprising nor coincidental.

Providing incentives for people to support themselves and improve their own lot is necessary for a society to thrive. Paul admonished the Thessalonians: "We were not idle when we were with you, nor did we eat anyone's food without paying for it. On the contrary, we worked night and day, laboring and toiling so that we would not be a burden to any of you. We did this, not because we do not have the right to such help, but in order to make ourselves a model for you to follow. For even when we were with you, we gave you this rule: 'If a man will not work, he shall not eat.'" (2 Thes 3:7–10)

Paul was not being malicious or uncharitable. He was not saying that help should be withheld from anyone truly in need. He was simply stating the obvious fact that people need to be productive. Productive people are the strength of a society, and accumulation of wealth and capital allows people not only to care for their own families, but also to be charitable and to enhance their productivity through education and labor-saving capital.

Poverty has become a relative concept, and the modern definition is based on aggregating people on the basis of a set of criteria determined by a bureaucrat. The poor in real life, however, are real individual people who make choices.

An encouraging aspect of poverty in America is that there is a significant level of mobility between the income categories.[22] According to a report by Robert Rector, *Understanding and Reducing Poverty in America*,[23] a significant percentage of the poor move to higher income levels over a period of years. While a small percentage of the poor are truly unable to fend for themselves, it is arrogant and foolish to view all poor people as helpless and dependent. This is especially so with the modern definition of poverty that includes many who are outside any rational or biblical understanding of true poverty.

According to the Rector report, cited above, the modern definition of poverty gives the following results:

—Forty-six percent of all poor households actually own their own homes. The average home owned by persons classified as poor by the Census Bureau is a three-bedroom house with one-and-a-half baths, a garage, and a porch or patio.

—Seventy-six percent of poor households have air conditioning. By contrast, 30 years ago, around 1980, only 36 percent of the entire U.S. population enjoyed air conditioning.

—Only 6 percent of poor households are overcrowded. More than two-thirds have more than two rooms per person.

—The average poor American has more living space than the average individual living in Paris, London, Vienna, Athens, and other cities throughout Europe. (These comparisons are to the average citizens in foreign countries, not to those classified as poor.)

—Nearly three-quarters of poor households own a car; 30 percent own two or more cars.

---

[22] "Income Mobility in the U.S. 1996 to 2005." Report of the Department of the Treasury, 2007

[23] Robert E. Rector, *Understanding and Reducing Poverty in America*, Testimony before the Joint Economic Committee of the United States Senate, available at www.heritage.org.

—Ninety-seven percent of poor households have a color television; over half own two or more color televisions.

—Seventy-eight percent have a VCR or DVD player; 62 percent have cable or satellite TV reception.

—Seventy-three percent own microwave ovens, more than half have a stereo, and a third have an automatic dishwasher.

The report goes on to summarize: "Overall, the typical American defined as poor by the government has a car, air conditioning, a refrigerator, a stove, a clothes washer and dryer, and a microwave. He has two color televisions, cable or satellite TV reception, a VCR or DVD player, and a stereo. He is able to obtain medical care. His home is in good repair and is not overcrowded. By his own report, his family is not hungry and he had sufficient funds in the past year to meet his family's essential needs. While this individual's life is not opulent, it is equally far from the popular images of dire poverty conveyed by the press, liberal activists, and politicians."

There are obviously some people who are desperately poor and incapable of taking care of themselves, but poverty statistics and analyses have a great deal of politics involved, a fact that tends to skew the results.

Many people make life choices that affect their standard of living. While they may make less money because of those choices, it doesn't necessarily mean they are destitute and miserable. Various cultural groups, such as the Amish religious sects, choose to forgo many of the conveniences and labor-saving innovations of modern society. They have few conveniences, and their children run around barefoot all summer. It is preposterous, however, to classify them in the same category as a destitute family in a Nigerian slum earning a dollar a day.

The Amish live full, abundant lives of their own choosing. They have to work hard from the time they are children, but it is arrogant to say that they are not happy simply because they don't live the lifestyle that a bureaucrat says they should.

A typical American married couple starts off with a low income and scrapes by trying to raise a young family. As they learn new valuable skills and get established in careers, their income increases. As they grow older, they join the ranks of the middle class. If they have been thrifty and wise in their planning, they may have a significant amount accumulated for retirement. Thus, they may progress through various income levels as they continue their life journey. That is a very typical scenario in a free society.

Many of the people designated as poverty-stricken in the United States and other developed countries cannot be classified as poor based on biblical principles. While they may be less well off relative to others, that relative difference is not poverty in the same sense as families living on one dollar a day in less developed countries. When Jesus discussed the poor and the Christian responsibility toward them, he was talking about the paralytics, orphans, and old widows who had no source of sustenance. They are the primary and appropriate targets of Christian charity.

A society develops when free people have the incentives to behave as the wife of noble character in Proverbs 31:10–31, reprinted on pages 69–70. As more people prosper, there is less true poverty and more potential for charitable people to act as the wife of noble character does, "She opens her arms to the poor, and extends her hands to the needy."

21. Property

So Ephron's field in Machpelah near Mamre–both the field and the cave in it, and all the trees within the borders of the field,–was deeded to Abraham as his property. (Gn 23:17–18)

Property is wealth. Without property, there can be no prosperity. Ownership is the title and right to the exclusive use and control of property. Possession itself does not constitute ownership, but it is a key attribute of ownership. "Thou shall not steal" is a direct command for the recognition of every individual's right to property.

"The Noblest Triumph,"[24] written by Tom Bethell, is a history of private property. Mr. Bethell asserts that most historians and many economists overlook the importance of private property as the cornerstone for development of society. As people who lived, and still live, in communist regimes and under violent dictators can attest, there is little meaning or significance of any other rights without the right to own property.

You are at the mercy of the ruling class when you are dependent on them for everything. Bethell refers to Leon Trotsky, a leading Soviet Communist revolutionary, who said: "where there is no private ownership, individuals can be bent to the will of the state, under threat of starvation."[25] It is only when people can provide for themselves that they are able to be independent and possess the power to practice their other freedoms.

This is important for the topic of this book, because property is

---

[24] Tom Bethell, *The Noblest Triumph,* (New York: St. Martin's Griffin, 1998).

[25] Bethell, 9.

the only way for poor societies to break from the cycle of poverty. For more than a decade, several organizations have produced similar reports ranking all countries of the world that have information available, based on the level of economic freedom.[26,27] The various indexes of economic freedom have shown a remarkable correlation between economic freedom and the standard of living and well being of the members of the various societies, including the poor.

Correlation is not causality, but it is convincing support of the principle that economic freedom increases the overall well-being of the people in a society. Property ownership and institutions that protect it are important criteria of the indexes. Since many of the policies of churches and government bodies deal with the poor and developing countries, it is important to have a solid understanding of the factors that actually cause the level of poverty or well being to increase or decrease.

Peruvian economist Hernando de Soto and the Institute for Liberty and Democracy have done extensive research in various countries in an attempt to understand the causes of progress and poverty, and summarized it in his book *The Mystery of Capital*.[28]

The primary findings of his book center on the idea that the difference between prosperous "Western" nations and poorer developing nations is the conception of property. The West includes those countries that have societies and economies based on Anglo-American, free market philosophies, no matter where in the world they are located. Thus, countries such as Australia are included in the group of countries called "the West."

---

[26] James D. Gwartney and Robert Lawson, *Economic Freedom*.

[27] Ambassador Terry Miller and Kim R. Holmes, Ph.D., *Index of Economic Freedom*, (Washington, D.C.: Heritage Foundation and New York: Dow Jones and Company, Inc., 2009). http://www.heritage.org/index/Download.aspx, also available in print.

[28] Henando de Soto, *The Mystery of Capital*, (New York: Basic Books, 2000)

He found that property in the West is formalized. There are formal titles to many types of property, and the titles are legally defensible. This strong protection of property enables owners to use it for building more capital, which increases productivity to a greater extent. The legal systems in place make it relatively easy to transfer title in trade, to borrow money with property as collateral, and to protect it against the depredations of others.

Third-world countries, on the other hand, have a weak concept of private property, lack an effective legal system for protecting it, and are smothered by bureaucratic monsters that throw roadblocks in front of anyone trying to start or maintain a business.

This state of affairs in poorer countries has profound ramifications. Since production is the source of all wealth, and since capital investments by entrepreneurs are the engines of production, the lack of strong formal property rights severely restricts the ability of the people to lift themselves out of poverty through wealth creation.

A focus on poverty reduction that does not address the structural causes of poverty is bound to fail and wastes a tremendous amount of resources. Property should be of primary importance in dealing with third-world countries. In nearly all cases, the people labor under the burden of dictators or a predatory ruling class.

There are startling contemporary examples of successful and prosperous nations falling back into destitution because the institutions of property and its legal structure were dismantled. The most striking modern example is the nation of Zimbabwe. Not long ago, it was called the breadbasket of Africa. It had excess agricultural produce that it would export to others in the area. Whatever the faults may have been with the prior social order, a system was in place that protected property and allowed trade and capital to be effectively utilized in production.

Starting in the year 2000, the Zimbabwe government imposed a massive land-redistribution scheme that destroyed property rights of the productive farmers, most of whom were white. It was rationalized on the basis of past injustices from colonial times. Whether or not the dispossession was politically justifiable, the outright destruction of property rights destroyed the economy. The incentives to production and capital improvement have been dismantled. The productive infrastructure has crumbled, and the country has since been in a state of crisis, with maize (corn) and wheat production cut to one tenth of its level in the year 2000. The people continually faced mass starvation and hyperinflation until the currency crumbled and foreign currencies were used for trade.

Haiti, the poorest country in the Western Hemisphere, is also a demonstration of what happens when corrupt government and lack of protection for individual rights prevent progress. It has been named the 3rd-most-corrupt nation in the world by Transparency International. Corruption and bureaucracy make it difficult for even the most tenacious of entrepreneurs to start a formal productive business.

Hernando de Soto and his team set up an experiment in Lima, Peru, to determine what it would take for a poor person in that city to start a business legally.

"It took more than 300 days working six hours a day. The cost: thirty-two times the monthly minimum wage. We performed a similar experiment to find out what it would take for a person living in an extralegal housing settlement, whose permanence the government had already acknowledged, to acquire legal title to a home. To receive approval from only the municipality of Lima—just one of the eleven government agencies involved—took 728 bureaucratic steps."[29]

Thus, much of the Peruvian economy is informal and underground, because it takes far too much effort and resources to comply with the formal rules. Much of Peru remains mired in

---

[29] De Soto, The Mystery of Capital, 190–199.

poverty.

This same scenario occurs in most third-world countries. Tyranny, corruption, and bureaucratic walls separate the poor from any hope of access to the legal markets. The economies of the poor countries are, in large measure, informal, with weak or nonexistent formal titles to property, constantly subject to confiscation by various methods.

This would seem to be a proper and more effective focus of moral indignation on the part of the religious community. Breaking the grip of injustice cannot occur if political tyranny and corruption abound. Lifting people out of poverty cannot occur without adequate protection of property rights and enhancing their ability to accumulate wealth without fear of confiscation or confiscatory taxation. See pages 184-187, "How Can I Make a Difference?" for things that you can do to be a part of the solution to the problem of oppression and the resulting poverty.

The commandments form a solid foundation for a Christian understanding of property rights. While we are called by God to be generous, we are also called to respect the rights of others to their belongings. As we shall see in the next section, the very idea of justice in Judeo-Christian theology is founded on the Ten Commandments. Injustice arises when the rights of the people under the commandments are abused.

22. Justice

For the Lord gives wisdom, and from his mouth come knowledge and understanding. He holds victory in store for the upright, he is a shield to those whose walk is blameless, for he guards the course of the just and protects the way of his faithful ones. Then you will understand what is right and just and fair – every good path. (Prv 2:6–9)

Justice is a theme throughout much of the Bible. It is also an important theme in contemporary pronouncements from church and state. It is a nebulous term, however, and is often misunderstood and distorted by very loose thinking. It is necessary to develop an understanding of what it means in order to apply it to everyday situations.

The poor were quite powerless in ancient times, even more so than those who are considered poor now, at least those in developed countries. Though they had property, the institutions of the day did not protect the poor very well. "A poor man's field may produce abundant food, but injustice sweeps it away." (Prv 13:23)

It was most often abusive rulers who did the unjust sweeping, because they could do so without much resistance from the poor or outrage from the rich citizens. Those who were well off had little care or compassion for the poor. The poor were considered wretched sinners by many and not worthy of much effort to defend.

Psalm 82 calls upon righteous people to "Defend the cause of the weak and fatherless, maintain the rights of the poor and oppressed. Rescue the weak and needy; deliver them from the hand of the wicked." (Ps 82:3–4) This was the message that Jesus brought, a message that was startling to the leading citizens of his

106

day. Justice had to do with protecting the rights of everyone.

That meant that justice should be weighed not by the level of prosperity but by the requirements of the commandments. "When you give testimony in a lawsuit, do not pervert justice by siding with the crowd, and do not show favoritism to a poor man in his lawsuit." (Ex 23:2–3) "Do not deny justice to your poor people in their lawsuits. Have nothing to do with a false charge . . . ." (Ex 23:6) People should be honest in their dealings and in their testimony, from the poorest to the wealthiest.

Justice, from the earliest biblical times, meant not taking what doesn't belong to you, not lying or giving false testimony, not murdering or injuring someone, not using force or fraud to get what you want. Justice had to do with respecting the rights of everyone, without regard to class or wealth. The rights were defined by the Ten Commandments. Injustice is not following the direction of the commandments, but rather trampling the rights of the poor, and oppressing the weak. Oppression came from the political class, those with power to force compliance. Injustice came from using false weights and measures, from the powerful taking what was not theirs, from cheating and fraud, and from perverting the courts from upholding what was right and just.

Jesus had scathing criticism for the politicians of his time, criticism that ultimately led to his death on the Cross. They could not accept the words of Jesus because their entire lives were wrapped up in the culture of division and oppression. The good news of the gospel is that Jesus came to free his people from sin. He will come again to judge the just and the unjust, but as in times of the Bible, justice is still measured by whether the commandments of loving God and neighbor were followed. There is no other definition of justice for a Christian.

23. Oppression

Woe to those who make unjust laws, to those who issue oppressive decrees, to deprive the poor of their rights and withhold justice from the oppressed of my people, making widows their prey and robbing the fatherless. (Is 10:1–3)

Oppression is a major theme throughout the entire bible, but what does it mean to us? There are 130 references in the New International Version of the Bible to words that include "oppress," such as oppression and oppressor, an example of which heads this page. As with this verse, in almost all references where the oppressor is identified, it is a Pharaoh, a king, an enemy nation, the "wicked," or those who dwell on high (the ruling elite). Most others are references to the Princes of Israel or their priests, officials, prophets, robbers, and extorters.

Oppression comes ultimately from those with the power of the sword. As Ecclesiastes 5:8–9 points out, "If you see the poor oppressed in a district, and justice and rights denied, do not be surprised at such things; for one official is eyed by a higher one, and over them both are others higher still. The increase of the land is taken by all; the king himself profits from the fields."

Wealth, however, is only indirectly connected with that power. When wealth is attained by people only through voluntary trade, as is most wealth in a free society, it is not a source of oppression. It is the result of people serving others, of "market entrepreneurs." In opposition to that, not all trade is voluntary. There is a group of business people who may be classified as "political entrepreneurs," those who use the power of government to eliminate or hamper the competition, limit markets, manipulate prices, or enforce compliance. Political entrepreneurs work with government in a partnership of oppression in many developed, as well as undeveloped countries. They have existed for as long as government has.

The most egregious cases of oppression that we witness, the starvation or murder of millions of people, the collapse of economies, the destruction of rights, and the impoverishment of the politically weak, are inevitably done by the hands of an unrestricted, unlimited, brutal, and evil government. The ghastly, inhumane, and unthinkable horrors of the last century have all been done by political powers, which use the excuse that they are improving mankind. As Josef Stalin said, you need to break a few eggs to make an omelet.

With freedom there is no oppression. If government is severely limited to its role of punishing those who violate the rights of others, then only voluntary exchange will occur. By definition, oppression is the lack of freedom or of volition. It is the lack of the ability of individuals to make decisions for themselves. It is slavery in its various forms. All governments, whether in developed or undeveloped countries, engage in oppression when they deny the rights of the people to make choices for themselves. Whether or not the justification is the social good, as nearly all tyrants and dictators proclaim, the result is an oppressed people and harmful social and economic effects. In most developed societies, this oppression is limited by some type of constitutional framework, but that protective framework is weakening as oppression grows in even the most free countries of today.

24. Good Government

If a ruler listens to lies, all his officials become wicked. (Prv 29:12)

When the righteous thrive, the people rejoice: but when the wicked rule, the people groan. (Prv 29:2)

People have a variety of ideas about what government should do and what makes a good government. The Apostle Paul gave a description of good government: "For rulers hold no terror for those who do right," (Rom 13:3) and: "For he is God's servant, to do you good." (Rom 13:4) If he does not do good or punishes people for doing good or doesn't punish people for doing evil, then he is not acting as God's servant. The verses at the top of the page are explicit recognition that evil governments existed and were not God's servants.

It is beyond reason to believe that Adolph Hitler, Josef Stalin, and Mao Zedong were God's agents, merely because they had wrested political power. It has been estimated that, together with other totalitarian dictators of the last century, they are responsible for the murder and deliberate starvation of well over 100 million people—men, women and children. They are not the kind of rulers that the Apostle Paul suggested that Christians submit to.

Paul said, "Therefore, it is necessary to submit to the authorities, not only because of possible punishment, but also because of conscience." (Rom 13:5) The point was not to follow bad rulers thoughtlessly down the road to destruction, but rather not to give non-Christians a reason to criticize Christians as lawless or evil. Christians were to "be ready to do whatever is good, to slander no one, to be peaceable and considerate, and to show humility toward all men." (Ti 3:1–2) They were to live in such a way that good rulers would commend them for their good behavior. It was because of conscience, however, that Paul defied authorities. It was because of conscience and defiance that Jesus and his followers were arrested, imprisoned, and put to death by the authorities. Many Christians have been whipped, beaten, imprisoned, starved, raped, tortured, fed to hungry lions, and murdered because they defied authorities. The defiance took place because the authorities were not doing what was right or good. The apostle James said, "Submit yourselves, then, to God. Resist the devil, and he will flee from you." (Jas 4:7) In Acts 5:29, "Peter and the other apostles replied: 'We must obey God rather than men!'" The Christians were persecuted because they were doing what was right and good, what God commanded them to do. They were resisting the devil, embodied in evil rulers.

History is filled with episodes of bad government. Good people have been punished because they did not agree with bad laws. Good people have been punished because they had the wrong color skin or the wrong family heritage, or belonged to the wrong religion. People were punished by government because they didn't worship the ruler or they objected to his confiscation or heavy burden of excessive taxes and regulations.

Good government does the same things that good people do. It does not steal, it is honest, open, and truthful in all of its dealings, it is fair in its rulings, it does not kill or destroy, it does not covet. Good government is bound to the same requirements that the Commandments impose on individuals. Authorities are God's servants and governments are good when they don't do evil themselves.

Jesus said "Give to Caesar what is Caesar's." (Mt 22:21) Many people view that as the explicit justification of any level of taxation by any government for any purpose. If you read the phrase in the context that it was given, however, it is obvious that that is not the proper interpretation. As was their usual tactic, the Pharisees were trying trap Jesus with words. They were using a rhetorical trick to box him in, to make him say something for which they could arrest him. Jesus' words were not a profound lesson on universal truth. His reply was a rhetorical escape. The full context of the exchange is as follows:

"But Jesus, knowing their evil intent, said, 'You hypocrites, why are you trying to trap me? Show me the coin used for paying the tax.' They brought him a denarius, and he asked them, 'Whose portrait is this? And whose inscription?' 'Caesar's,' they replied. Then he said to them, 'Give to Caesar that which is Caesar's, and to God what is God's'" The rhetoric was not a theological justification for taxation, but rather a clever answer to a logical bind.

Much of the Old Testament is written about how God delivered his people from the hands of the oppressors, the bad authorities, and unjust government. Oppressive and unjust government exists on a wide scale even today. God has always called his people to resist evil and to free the oppressed from their rulers. He calls Christians now to proclaim the truth of the gospel and not to give in to what is wrong, even if that wrong is given the face of government and politicians.

The job of resisting evil and oppression is as difficult and daunting today as it ever was. Powerful, centralized governments use their enormous power to ensnare the people and bind heavy burdens on them. Even worse, some people are encouraging government to act as the savior and provider of all good things, forsaking the message of God throughout the Bible.

We, as Christians, are commanded to be truthful, to be satisfied with what is ours, not to covet the things of others, to be fair and kind, not to injure others, and to live the kind of lives that good rulers would commend. He also called us to speak the truth of the gospel, to truly care for those in need, to follow and teach the commandments of loving God and neighbor.

Part 3

Discussion of Policy Prescriptions

25. Policy Prescriptions

It is not good to have zeal without knowledge, nor to be hasty and miss the way. (Prv 19:2)

The work of Christian churches is to carry on the message and the work of the gospel of Jesus Christ. There are various ways of doing that and ample opportunities to continue that work.

One of the ways that many churches pursue the mission of the gospel is through policy prescriptions for their members or for elected officials. The prescriptions often have to do with the way church members are to live their lives or the laws that politicians are supposed to pass in order to bring about the conditions to fulfill the requirements of the gospel.

The problem with many of the policy prescriptions is that they are "rules of men," as Jesus said, and not the will of God. They may be based on good intentions that have a ring of plausibility, but they defy economic law and the reality of God's world and thus, are destined to hurt more people than they help. Defying physical or economic law will result in harm, no matter how good the intentions are.

Part 3 is an analysis of specific policy prescriptions from the perspective of economic law. Some prescriptions are merely useless and misguided, while others cause serious damage and hurt the very people they are purporting to help. The aim of these analyses is not to criticize the people who think this way, because most people truly are sincere in their concern for others. The aim is to draw attention to the fact that their actions have real implications according to God's natural law, implications that may give very different results than what they expect or desire. The real issue is often not so much the action that is proposed, but rather that the proposal is to use the coercion of government to enforce the prescription. The compulsion leads to perverse results and is entirely against the gospel of Jesus.

Typically, if the actions were beneficial to the participants, they would do them without compulsion. If the actions do not benefit the participants, it is immoral and unethical to force them to participate. If the laws of the government are used only to prevent one citizen from taking actions that injure others, that is within the limited definition of good government and is merely a reflection of the requirements of the Commandments, as well as most other moral code. Good government does not conflict with Christian requirements.

The primary problem with using government force beyond restraining the abuses of rights is that economic relationships are distorted. The good results expected from voluntary cooperation are prevented and bad results are enhanced. The issues listed on the following pages are a small sampling of the many policies that promote discord and negative effects. Each will be discussed separately to get a good overview of the problems. This is, by no means, a complete list. Many others are similar and a comparable analysis could be conducted on each of them.

26. Policy Prescriptions That Hurt

1. Egalitarianism
2. Minimum Wage / Living Wage
3. Price Gouging Regulations / Price Controls
4. Fair Trade
5. Public Education
6. Buy Local / Buy American / Self Sufficiency
7. Stop Evictions Now
8. Welfare / Redistribution programs
9. Socialized Medicine / Universal Health Care
10. Insurance Regulation
11. International Development Programs
12. Kyoto Protocol / Global Warming Legislation
13. Money and Inflation

27. Egalitarianism

Do not pervert justice; do not show partiality to the poor or favoritism to the great, but judge your neighbor fairly. (Lv 19:15)

Egalitarianism is the ideal that everyone should be equal. It does not mean equal in the sense of equal treatment under the law, regardless of skin color, height, gender, religion, or level of wealth. It means that everyone ends up the same. It means that everyone finishes the race together, even if that entails placing heavy weights on the faster runners.

Many people assume that egalitarianism is the moral high ground, that inequality of conditions is inherently bad, and that social equality equals justice. To the contrary, however, egalitarianism is the repudiation of reason, of all of economics, of the Bible, of the commandments and morality, of human intelligence, and of life itself.

It is quite evident that no two situations are alike. Someone who chooses to live in the desert will have certain resources that are available and specific limitations as to what he or she can produce. The same person doing the same thing in fertile valleys or in a rain forest or in the Arctic tundra will have a different set of resources and limitations.

Obviously, geographic location will give certain advantages and disadvantages, unequal productivity and unequal wealth for identical people in each of those situations. That is neither bad nor good. It just is. To say it shouldn't be is like saying that gravity shouldn't exist.

When you consider the vast differences in intellect, native

talent, size, dexterity, and a thousand other attributes of human beings, the large differences due to geography are magnified. Some people are exceptionally bright, some are exceptionally dull. Again, that is not good or bad, it just is. It is nature, it is life.

Some people in society are surgeons. No matter how brilliant the individual is, becoming a surgeon doesn't happen accidentally or automatically. A person becomes a surgeon by making a decision to pay the very high price to get there. While the monetary cost is high, there are far more important costs to take into consideration. It takes many years of grueling study, hard work, long hours, and unpleasant conditions to make it to the point where a physician can excel at his or her work. It is a price that many smart, competent people are not willing to pay. That is true, to some extent, for almost any profession. There are many capable people who choose not to pay the personal price and, in so doing, choose a lower-paying career.

Some unfortunate souls who have paid the price find out after the fact that the ongoing personal cost is not worth the higher pay. The author knows a successful engineer, for example, who didn't want the rat race any longer. He gave up an engineer's salary to become a farmer. His income was less, and farming was harder, more-dangerous physical work and required longer hours, but, to him, it was worth it. He made a tradeoff because he valued some things more than a high salary. Not everyone agrees with him, and many people wouldn't make the choice he did. We can see from this example, though, that much more enters into the picture than just innate abilities or geography.

All human beings make tradeoffs in their daily lives that affect the future. Students at all levels of education take actions each day that affect their future, their careers, and their lives. There are some who are not exceptionally intelligent, but they work very hard and become exceptional. There are others who have a high level of native intelligence and skill, but they choose not to use them for whatever reason. It is reasonable to expect that the economic results of those two will likely be significantly different.

In general, those with higher intelligence, those with specific valuable innate skills and attributes, and those who work harder and longer will earn more money and be able to do things that those less intelligent or less skilled or less hard working will not. That is very good because it rewards people for being productive, thus contributing to the well being of all.

What is bad is when people take things that do not belong to them. Theft and physical aggression, whether actual or threatened, are almost universally thought of as bad. Throughout history, morality has centered on respect for the life and property of the individual. The commandments, which are the foundation of all Christian ethics and morality, include "Thou shall not steal" and "Thou shall not murder" and "Thou shall not covet."

Further, what is immoral for one person to do is also immoral for presidents, congressmen, or any collection of people to do. Throughout the Bible, God's people are admonished to free the oppressed. The biggest, most effective predators and oppressors in modern times are large centralized governments, who use the flag of equality to cover their sins and to justify massive legalized theft, interference in the lives of citizens, and even mass murder.

Jesus commanded us to love our neighbor, feed the poor, house the homeless, and to give drink to the thirsty. It is the calling of Christians to participate in that mission. The command that Jesus gave, however, in no way gave governments authority to take from one to give to another. His command did not, in any sense, call on Christians to take money or resources by force or coercion to use for their charity, or to use the laws or institutions of society for that purpose.

The parable of the Good Samaritan is the model for charity. (Lk 10:30–37) The Samaritan did not jump the passersby who followed him and force them with the point of a sword to take care of the man who was robbed and beaten. He took him to be cared for and paid for it out of his own pocket. That is the message of Christian charity. That is the entire message of the gospel. That is the love that Jesus became a model for.

When Jesus talked about caring for the poor, the hungry, the naked, or the homeless, he was always talking to individuals. The Roman army occupied the territory, but mostly left the Israelites alone as long as they paid their tribute and did not cause a stir. The real government of his day was made up of the Pharisees, Sadducees, teachers of the law, temple officials, and other Jewish leaders. Jesus recognized their injustice, legalized theft, and hypocrisy.

Many politicians of modern times are similar to the political leaders of his time. There is corruption and abuse of the rights of the people on a broad scale. There is no real concern of politicians for the true welfare of the people. There are only voting blocks to purchase with money taken from others.

Equality of conditions is a description of subsistence agricultural economies and stagnant socialist societies. There are some limited societies that appear to be living well under an officially egalitarian system. An example is the tiny island of Hime, off the coast of Japan.[30] Its inhabitants' primary source of income is fishing and shrimp farming. On closer inspection, however, their tiny egalitarian society was enabled by generous public works provided by non-egalitarian outsiders in return for being a loyal source of votes for the Liberal Democratic Party of Japan. It is sustained by trade with outside innovators and entrepreneurs who are free from egalitarian strangling.

It is quite obvious that, if that tiny island culture was used as a model for the rest of the world, all societies would be stagnant,

---

[30] A Worker's Paradise Found Off Japan's Coast, nytimes.com, The New York Times, April 22, 2009.

unproductive, subsistence economies with little innovation or development and mass poverty. The people of Hime are comfortable and don't want to rock the boat, but their comfort comes from the outside and is not a result of their enforced egalitarianism.

Innovation and improvement in the lives of the masses of people come about when the incentive to innovate is present. That incentive is profit. Naturally, those who innovate more, produce more, and make more lives better off will profit more. That is a very biblical principle. "Lazy hands make a man poor, but diligent hands bring wealth." (Prv 10:4) When Jesus was talking of the powerful centurion, a gentile with great authority and servants to serve him, he said: "I tell you the truth, I have not found anyone in Israel with such great faith." (Mt 8:10)

The fact is that God does not expect complete equality of circumstance. He expects faithfulness and trust in our daily lives. The Apostle Paul said, "For I have learned to be content whatever the circumstance. I know what it is like to be in need, and I know what it is to have plenty. I have learned the secret of being content in any and every situation, whether well fed or hungry, whether living in plenty or in want. I can do everything through him who gives me strength." (Phil 20:11–13)

That is, in essence, the message that Jesus came to deliver: Do not trust in riches, do not trust in governing officials, do not trust in your own cleverness. Trust in God.

28. Minimum Wage/Living Wage

Friend, I am not being unfair to you. Didn't you agree to work for a denarius? Take your pay and go. (Mt 20:13–16)

Minimum wages have been an emotional and volatile subject for many decades. The reason that the issue has been so emotional is that people base their opinions on what they think the world should be like, instead of understanding what it is like. Emotion gets in the way of understanding.

Most people are generous, caring, and helpful. They don't like to see people suffer. They don't like to see poverty. They want people to have a better life. That is a great positive quality of the typical Christian and, in fact, nearly all human beings. Christ calls us to care for the poor, feed the hungry, and to clothe the naked. Many people feel compelled to do something.

The frequent problem with people "doing something" is that those people don't really do something. They demand that government do something so they don't have to. Getting someone else to do something makes them feel better without having to get their hands dirty. The sad fact is that using government regulations to fight poverty is fundamentally flawed and always ineffective in the long run. Coercive manipulations of the markets cause economic distortions, which typically have worse effects than the original problem. As discussed in an earlier section, the economic laws are not compassionate. They don't bend to good intentions. They just explain the way the world works. If you drink gasoline because you think it will give you more energy, you will still likely die, because the laws of biology and chemistry are also not compassionate. The results follow from the cause.

It helps to understand that wages are simply the prices of the various labor services. There is no inherent difference from any other item in the economy. Just as there are different qualities and values of furniture or clothing, there are different qualities and values of labor. Therefore, labor is not a generic, catch-all category that lumps ditch diggers, secretaries, clerks, baseball players, and aeronautical engineers together. Each type of labor in each geographic area has a separate market that is related to the conditions of the locality and the people at a point in time.

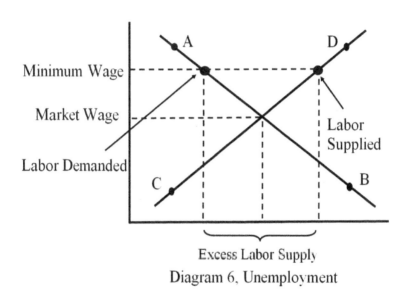

Diagram 6. Unemployment

Similar to every good and service, the price or wage of a particular skill in a particular market is determined by the number of people attempting to supply that skill in relation to the number of people that employers or customers need for that particular skill. As discussed under Prices in Part 1, the market clearing price is that at which the number of hours of that service that people are willing and able to provide equals the number of hours of that service that others are willing and able to buy. At that price, there will be no excess supply of labor, called unemployment, nor excess demand for labor, called labor shortages.

Minimum wages are a legal requirement for employers to pay no less than a given price per hour for any employee service. The idea arises out of good intentions, the desire to help poor people. The reason that the idea fails to reduce poverty is that it ignores all economic law and uses the force of government to distort economic reality. A minimum wage is price fixing in the labor markets. When it is at or below the market wage, it has no effect. In order to keep good employees from migrating to competing firms, an employer will need to pay the market-determined price for the service.

On the other hand, if the minimum price of the skill is above the market wage for that skill, the effect is to increase the number of people competing for the available jobs and to decrease the jobs available. The quantity of labor supplied increases while the quantity demanded decreases. The inevitable result is a glut of labor, an excess supply that is known as unemployment of participants in that particular market.

The perverse result of minimum-wage laws is that they don't help the poor in any significant way, in spite of good intentions. In 2003, only 9% of minimum-wage workers were heads of poor households according to a study by professors Richard V. Burkhauser and Joseph J. Sabia.[31] It does, however, hurt the young, the unskilled, and the new job-seekers the most. To understand why, we need to recognize that an employer competing in a market will not hire someone if the anticipated marginal revenue, the additional

---

[31] Raising New York's Minimum Wage: Another Empty Promise to the Working Poor, by Richard V. Burkhauser and Joseph J. Sabia, 2004, a study conducted for the Employment Policies Institute, p. 1. Burkhauser is a professor at Cornell University, Sabia is a professor at the University of Georgia.

sales generated by the employee's work, is not greater than the marginal cost of employing him or her. It just wouldn't make sense to do so.

Low-skill jobs attract low-skill workers because they are not qualified to perform higher-skilled jobs. Those employees with more valuable skills would tend to migrate to higher-skill jobs, because they can earn more money there. Again, that makes sense. Those with a higher skill-level are able to generate a higher marginal revenue or lower marginal costs from their services. An employer would be willing to pay more for an employee who can contribute more to profits. Therefore, higher-skilled people are generally not competitors for low-skill, low-wage jobs.

If, instead, wage levels for low-skill jobs were maintained at artificially high rates by law, they will attract more workers, those who would avoid the job at a lower wage. In addition, if an employer is going to have to pay a higher price anyway, the employer will prefer a more skilled person over one less skilled, because the employer will have more flexibility in assigning duties. A particular job is worth only the incremental profit that it brings to the employer. If the higher minimum wage raises the cost of the labor above the additional revenue that it brings to the employer, it doesn't make sense to continue employing someone for the position, and the job may be cut.

The net effect is that, not only will the low-skilled worker have more competition due to higher minimum wages, employers will have a lower demand for labor and will take lower-skilled workers only if no higher-skilled workers are available for the price. The very low-skill worker will be priced out of the market.

It is obvious what would happen if government regulation set a minimum price of automobiles at $20,000. There would be an immediate shift away from low-cost cars. The only cars that people would buy for $20,000 are those that are worth at least $20,000. Cars that previously sold for $12,000, $15,000, or $18,000 would just sit on the lot, even though there would be many customers willing to buy them at the lower cost.

In the same way, there are people with low-value skill sets. They are typically young workers, new to the market, with little experience to bring to the job. They have skills that people would be willing to pay a relatively low price for, but beyond that price, they might as well hire someone with a higher skill set who can be more productive, or not hire anyone at all.

While every human being has inherent dignity before God, the operation of economic law has nothing to do with dignity or malice or any other emotional quality. It has to do with reality, the way things actually work in God's ordered world. By setting the price of their services above their productivity, they are destined to sit on the lot, the unemployment line in human terms, just as those lower-priced, but still usable automobiles sit on the car lot under automobile price-fixing.

The effect of raising the minimum wage is that people with skills that aren't worth the price will not be hired or will lose their jobs. In spite of the good intentions of "helpful" people, low-skilled workers will be displaced by higher-skilled workers or technology improvements, and fewer people will be hired overall. Unemployed youth with no developed skills will find it harder to land that first job to get skills. Poor people with low-value skills will find it much harder to compete for a job and build up skills to make them more valuable.

That is, in fact, what happens. Burkhauser and Sabia found that, even though the minimum wage is purported to help the working poor, a large portion of the increase in wages due to the minimum goes to families far above the poverty level.[32] The reason is that low-wage jobs are typically entry-level, part-time jobs, not intended

---

[32] *Raising New York's Minimum Wage: A Poor Way to Help the Working Poor,* Richard V. Burkhauser and Joseph J. Sabia, 2004, a study conducted for the Employment Policies Institute, p. 3 .

to be permanent career positions. Second earners and college students, whose families already have significant income, are drawn into competition for lower-skill jobs by the higher pay.

In a separate study, Burkhauser and Sabia say that "the minimum wage is a poor policy tool to reduce poverty because most individuals earning the minimum wage do not live in families with low incomes."[33] A mother with children in a higher-income family may not consider taking a job if she doesn't have higher-value skills, because the cost of child care offsets too much of the earned income, and she would have to spend more time away from her family. On the other hand, if prices for her skills are artificially boosted, it may make sense for her to pay for child care and take the job. Thus, competition for the work increases.

There are various episodes throughout history where the impact is quite evident. In the1930s, it was common to see elevator operators. It was a low-skill, low-pay job, but it met the needs of some people. Automatic elevators were available at that time, but their high cost gave a relative advantage to the low-cost elevator operator. After the minimum wage of the 1930s made the elevator operator uncompetitive, within a couple of years, the job was obsolete. Automatic elevators got the advantage and the operators lost their jobs.

The same is true for gas-station attendants. Years ago, when you pulled into any gas station, an attendant pumped your gas, checked your oil, and washed your windows. The people who pumped gas were generally school boys out to earn a few extra dollars part-time, retired people supplementing their income, or others who felt that the low wage was worth their time. If they didn't think that it was worth their time, they wouldn't have taken the job. The gas-station attendant is now a relic of times gone by, not because people didn't want them, but because minimum wages gave automated gas pumps

---

[33] Burkhauser and Sabia, Raising New York's Minimum Wage, p. 2.

a competitive advantage.

Christians are called to help the poor. Saying you are helping, however, doesn't mean that you are really helping, unless the actions you take really give the results you expect. A study by Professors Richard K. Vedder and Lowell E. Gallaway on the relationship between minimum-wage laws and poverty concluded that "there is virtually no meaningful evidence that higher minimum wages reduce poverty in the United States."[34]

The flaw in minimum-wage arguments is the same flaw that arises in discussions whenever the government fixes prices or manipulates supply and demand, whether it be wages, wheat, or gasoline. Manipulating the market always leads to negative consequences because confused price signals distort the decision-making process of market participants. A minimum price above the market-clearing price will lead to gluts, a maximum price below the market-clearing price will lead to shortages.

The level of poverty and every other measure of well being are statistically correlated to the level of economic freedom.[35] For people who really have concern for the poor, the most effective actions would be, first, press to remove government from the economy so the general level of welfare will rise. Second, get their hands dirty and actually do something for the poor instead of just saying righteous things and demanding that the government take care of it using money taken from others.

---

[34] *Does Minimum Wage Reduce Poverty?*, Richard K. Vedder and Lowell E. Gallaway, Employment Policies Institute, June 2001, p. 16. Dr. Vedder and Dr. Galloway are both distinguished professors of economics at Ohio University.

[35] Gwartney and Lawson, *Economic Freedom*, xxii.

29. Price Controls/Gouging Regulations

There was a great famine in the city; the siege lasted so long that a donkey's head sold for eighty shekels [thirty two ounces] of silver, and a quarter of a cab [about a pint] of seed pods for five shekels[two ounces]. (2 Kgs 6:25)

Price gouging is another emotionally charged term, which people use when the price of a product or service is higher than the price they are used to paying. Somehow, politicians and state attorneys general think they can magically discern what the price of every commodity and service should be at any particular point in time. As we have seen already, a price shouldn't be at any set level. It is only a market signal that indicates that: 1) the number of buyers equals the number of sellers, 2) the number of buyers is less than the number of sellers, or 3) the number of buyers is greater than the number of sellers.

Referring to diagram 3 on page 36 in our discussion on prices, the price of any item in a free market is that point at which the number of sellers willing and able to sell approximately equals the number of buyers willing and able to buy. Supply and demand will be fairly well balanced at that point. If there is a severe shortage of any item due to external forces, such as a natural disaster, it is reasonable and expected that the price of that item should rise significantly and quickly.

A prime example is the occurrence of a major hurricane. Suddenly, the supplies of fresh water become contaminated, rendering it dangerous for human consumption. Supplies of building materials are destroyed, as are roads and means of transporting new products to the area. Hotels are destroyed, making rooms for rent scarce. In addition, demand for these things increases because the obvious need for repairs is great. People who lost their homes need somewhere to stay, so more hotel rooms are required.

When you combine the large increase in demand with the large decrease in supply for products and services, the result will be a significant spike in prices. As with other things economic, this is neither good nor bad, it just is. It is merely a description of reality.

From an overall perspective, the price fluctuations serve as a method to allocate the scarce products to those who need them the most. When prices increase, people tend to buy less. If it is gasoline, they may take fewer trips to the shopping mall, they may car-pool to work, and so on. If it is hotel rooms, families might squeeze more people into a room instead of renting multiple rooms. If it is fresh water, they may drink less, produce their own by boiling, and otherwise reduce their need to buy.

By not buying that extra tank of gas, by not renting that extra room, by not buying that extra gallon of water, they are saving that gas, that room, and that water for someone else who would not have gotten it at all. If prices are held to artificially low levels, people tend to recognize the bargain and buy and consume more than normal, instead of less. This leads to shortages that can sometimes be critical.

Those of us who are old enough can remember the gasoline price controls of the 1970s. A significant memory of that time is that of cars lined up for blocks at the gas stations because there was little supply. As soon as price controls were lifted, the shortage evaporated. Lines quickly dissipated, and things got back to normal. In the area of housing, people in a number of cities face critical shortages of homes and apartments because of economic controls over rental and ownership of housing. In similar situations, the housing shortage vanishes when controls are lifted.

Supply, demand, and prices are in balance and automatically

adjust when the equilibrium is disturbed. If artificial controls are applied to one, the other two automatically and uncontrollably adjust. If prices are held to a level lower than the market price, whether by law or by coercion, the inevitable result will be a shortage, with long lines and angry people going without. This has been the complete and undeniable history of price controls, whenever, wherever, and however they occur. This is documented in the fascinating historical study mentioned previously, called *Forty Centuries of Wage and Price Controls.*[36]

World War II is sometimes described as a time when price controls were necessary. The war effort used a tremendous amount of resources and prices started to rise because of increasing scarcity. Scarcity, however, in and of itself, is not a shortage in the economic sense. The higher prices will mean that the quantity demanded will be lower, but as long as buyers and sellers are free to exchange voluntarily at any price, the quantity supplied will approach the level of the quantity demanded.

Most people of the time willingly put up with the war time price controls and with the rationing that inevitably followed it, because they thought that the war effort was very important. They figured that they were doing their part. Whether or not people accepted the controls, however, is beside the point when discussing their economic effects. The increasing prices that price controls were designed to counteract were the result of demand being greater than supply. The price controls led to a shortage, meaning that the quantity supplied was less than the quantity demanded. Shortages led to long lines and people going without, and that led to rationing, rationing led to hoarding and black markets for goods, and that led to criminalization of normal, rational economic behavior. Wars or any other disasters don't invalidate economic laws. Everything that happens is understandable in economic terms.

---

[36] Schuettinger and Butler, *Forty Centuries.*

The question might be asked: What if there were no price controls or rationing or anti-hoarding laws at that time? What would happen then? If people were allowed to sell to and buy from whomever they wanted on whatever terms they wanted, prices would have increased, which would have drawn more suppliers into the market, alleviating at least some of the scarcity. People who really didn't need specific goods, or needed less of them, would not buy so much. Those who had extra would have had the incentive to offer it for sale at a higher price and add to the supply. All of those actions would have mitigated some of the increase in price and alleviated the need for rationing.

Price-gouging laws are not direct price controls, but rather threats of punishment if the seller is found guilty. The problem with price-gouging laws is that nobody really knows what the cutoff price is for conviction. If a customer gets angry and reports the purported offender, it is likely that a prosecution will follow. The business owners are subject to extortion by potential customers and by politicians trying to look like knights in shining armor.

Hurricane Katrina was one of the worst natural disasters in recent American history, affecting much of the American South and devastating the city of New Orleans. On the very first day after it struck, the President of the United States, the governor of Louisiana, and the mayor of New Orleans all made the proclamation that any business caught price gouging would be dealt with severely. Price gouging was not defined and the punishment was not enumerated, but the ultimate and absolutely predictable effect was that severe shortages ensued. Years after it occurred, large areas of the city remained in shambles.

Major rebuilding efforts by charitable organizations were hampered by lack of building supplies. For several years, people would line up at four o'clock in the morning to await the arrival of a tractor-trailer load of building materials at the only building-supply store in one area. Those not lucky enough to get there first would have to await the next load on a different day. What should have been a boon for the construction industry was turned into a man-made disaster for the residents. Major disincentives to business prevented new suppliers and other businesses from establishing a presence there. People continued to suffer because government interference in markets prevented the return to normal conditions.

The threats of prosecution serve the same purpose as outright price controls in keeping prices well below the market price. Thus, they practically ensure shortages for the very same reason that direct controls do. The victims of disasters have to deal not only with the original destruction, but also the destruction of markets by politicians.

If the overall objective is the rapid recovery of a disaster area, a far more effective method would be for politicians to call on everyone to come and gouge as much as they can and to make as much profit as possible. Because entrepreneurs respond to profit opportunities, the area would soon be inundated with suppliers trying to get their share of the easy profit. That inundation would be the very increase in supply that would help the area recover and draw prices down to or below normal levels. When good intentions minimize profit opportunities, those good intentions hurt everyone they intend to help.

30. Fair Trade

You are to use accurate scales, an accurate ephah and an accurate bath. (Ez 45:10) [An ephah is slightly more than one half bushel, dry measurement, a bath is a similar volume in liquid measure, about 20 quarts]

Fair Trade is a large international movement, promoted by sincere people, dedicated to the objective of lifting the poor in underdeveloped countries out of their poverty. The idea behind it is that the price of a good should be at least high enough to cover the costs of producing it. It is a rational effort to empower people to take control of their own lives and make a positive difference. That desire and effort are admirable . The problem is that, in the long run, they will not bring about development of poor societies. The good intentions of the program's proponents cannot raise many people from poverty because it relies on economic fallacy in its main proposition.

Price is one of the most important concepts in economics because it is so powerful in explaining circumstances and determining outcomes. The price of any good or service depends on the relationship of the demand with the supply. It has nothing to do with the costs of production. The production costs only determine the minimum price at which a producer will be able to make a profit. Below that price, the business can't survive.

Each producer has a different set of costs, based on the processes, materials, and capital it uses. Those with the highest unit costs of production will have the hardest time surviving in the market. High production costs are an indication of inefficient processes and methods. The producer has discovered a process that will not work and must be changed.

In any market, the price is a signal to all of the participants. At a low price, lower profits will be earned. The least efficient producers will likely become unprofitable. If prices remain low for an extended period, those inefficient producers will be forced to leave the market. While that is unfortunate for the particular supplier at that time, the effect on the market is to reduce the available supply. The entire supply curve shifts to the left, as seen in diagram 7. With a reduced supply, prices tend to increase.

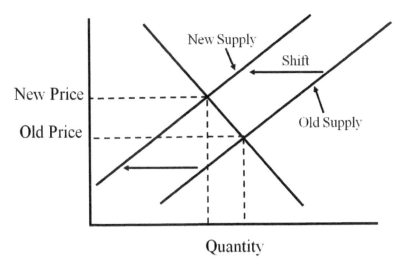

Diagram 7. Shift of Supply curve

The implications of this process are very important. As the least efficient producers leave the market, the excess supply disappears. The increased price that results means that the efficient producers who are left are more profitable than they were before. The higher profits mean that they have more money left over with which to buy other goods and services.

As discussed in the chapter on the division of labor, when various people specialize in different forms of production, they each become more productive. They can trade that excess productivity to others who also produce in excess of what they use. Coffee producers are a familiar and popular target of fair-trade programs, so we will use them as an example. Those coffee growers who were inefficient and went out of business would not be destined to unemployment and starvation, any more than are the non-farmers in America or any other developed nation.

Successful and profitable coffee growers can use their increased profits to buy new shoes. An inefficient coffee farmer may find he is a very good cobbler, making shoes that the profitable coffee growers would now be able to afford. Some people might learn how to grow vegetables or raise cattle efficiently, which will provide for those who specialize in making shoes or growing coffee. Some people might find they have a knack for carpentry. They can sell their carpentry services to the coffee growers, vegetable gardeners, and the cobblers, who can now afford higher quality buildings.

Fair trade, while it is based on good intentions, tends to distort the significance of true markets. It more firmly entrenches the subsistence agricultural economies because it attempts to prevent inefficient producers from failing. In any market economy, failure is a critical part of the improvement process. The least efficient producers remove themselves from competition and, instead, direct their efforts to activities for which they are better suited or more productive.

Of course it is a difficult time for families when they have to change occupations and maybe even locations. If they are free to do whatever it takes for them to ultimately succeed, it is likely that they will be better off in the long run than if they stayed where they were and struggled as a result of being the least efficient producer. Some farmers need to fail and leave overcrowded markets, but they also need other ready occupations at which they can be successful.

A major problem in developing countries where fair-trade programs are focused is that there are political barriers to access to formal markets by the poor. Bureaucratic regulations prevent entrepreneurs from establishing businesses and trying to serve others. Confiscatory taxes discourage the accumulation of capital and wealth. Lack of protection of property defeats the efforts of people to improve their lives. This is discussed in more depth in the chapters on Property (pages102-106) and Trade and Capital (pages 60-69)

If the desired result is development of society and less poverty in the long run, it would be far more effective to redirect resources, those devoted to promoting fair trade and higher prices for inefficient suppliers, toward efforts to change oppressive governments, to promote access to formal markets by the poor, to reduce bureaucratic obstacles and high regulatory costs for budding entrepreneurs, and to educate the poor in independent thinking, logical analysis, and problem solving.

It would be better for charitable organizations to provide aid and training in market research to determine what products would provide the most profitable niches. It would benefit the people if they fully understood that their choices determine their outcomes to a large extent. Educating them in saving and capital accumulation and working to preserve their rights to keep it, would give them a springboard from which they could jump to higher levels of well being for them and their communities.

It is important to encourage property ownership, the creation of personal wealth, innovation, the use of capital equipment for increased productivity and profits, and to let those markets develop that can better serve the expanded needs of the profitable, efficient providers. In the long run, any economy, and the people of which it is comprised, will benefit from diversifying away from dependence on subsistence farming toward trade of goods and services, where everyone can develop his or her own particular set of skills toward meeting the needs of others.

31. Public Education

Blessed is the man who finds wisdom, the man who gains understanding, for she is more profitable than silver and yields better returns than gold. She is more precious than rubies; nothing you desire can compare with her. Long life is in her right hand; in her left hand are riches and honor. (Prv 3:17)

Education is an important ingredient for progress in any society. It is a way to pass down knowledge gained from one generation to the next. Just as the accumulation of capital by people in society builds on the gains and progress of their forebears, so the accumulation of knowledge builds on the foundation laid in prior generations.

Newton's laws of physics are not invalidated because they are old. They are validated every day because they are true. They have not even been succeeded by the theory of relativity, but rather, relativity is an expansion of theory that is able to explain a wider range of phenomena, including the subset of Newtonian physics. Scientists of all kinds build upon the knowledge of giants before them, rather than building their own understanding from scratch.

There are many types of knowledge, and the value of that knowledge is based upon all of the laws of economics that determine the value of any good or service. That knowledge that grants its possessors the ability to solve big problems will generally be worth a big price. That knowledge that is very difficult to accumulate will ensure that those who take the time and mental effort will run into less competition, because few people are willing to pay the price in time and effort. That knowledge and skill that is easily acquired will be common, and thus the supply will be high relative to the demand. That means the price of that skill or knowledge in the marketplace will be low.

The importance that anyone attaches to an education depends on that person's assumptions and view of the future, as well as on his or her perceived capability to achieve at higher levels. Even in the poorest areas of the poorest countries in the world, families have established low-cost private schools and pay for them out of their own earnings. This is often in spite of having free government-provided schools close by. The poor want the best for their children and realize that the government monopoly in education often does not meet their expectations for their own children.

Professor James Tooley is a specialist in international development and education, and has written a book called *The Beautiful Tree*.[37] It is as much an indictment of the international-development community, which threw up continual roadblocks to his efforts, as it was about the resilience and hope of the poor. It is the culmination of years of work by research teams in some of the most poverty-stricken areas of the world. It is a narrative of people who, in spite of immense personal difficulty, made the decision to use some of their very scarce resources to provide a better education for their children.

It is a story of hope and determination, but it is also a very important lesson that education doesn't end if government does not provide schools. Education is a service that people value. If people are left to their own devices, they will get those things that they value. Public education is only one route to the education of our children. There are many other alternatives.

While many people see public education as a basic human right, it truly is only a service that people use. If it is valuable to them,

---

[37] James Tooley, *The Beautiful Tree* (Cato Institute, Washington D.C., 2009).

they will buy it. If they can't afford to buy it, there are a great many charitable people and organizations that could help to provide for them. Throughout history, charitable organizations have provided education to the poor. To say that people would fall through the cracks in a totally private, voluntary system is to ignore the hoards of students falling through the cracks in the profoundly failing public-school system. In numerous cities, the graduation rate for all students is around 50%, not a particularly encouraging statistic.

The government near-monopoly in education, in America and most other developed countries, involves the involuntary taking of money from taxpayers to provide a service. As with any service, monopoly provision under coercive terms leads to gross inefficiency. Government bureaucracy makes public education very expensive, rigid, and ineffective. Even though the public schools are paid for by taxes that they still have to pay, many parents are opting out and paying additional money for private education, or home schooling their children, because they believe that public schools are failing them and miseducating their children, similar to the desperately poor families in India and sub-Saharan Africa.

While education is important to people and society, it is no more important than food, clothing, or shelter, in fact, obviously less so. The arguments for public education fall apart when you recognize that everything important to the development of people, families and societies is and has been provided for, now and in all previous times, without the involvement of government. The fact that it is important is not a valid argument for provision of a service by coercion of the state.

The assumption that mandatory public education is necessary to provide for the poor is an argument for the taking of tax money through government coercion from one group to give to another group. It is based on the idea that the poor cannot provide for their own education and must rely on free government schools. This idea is destroyed in reality by Professor Tooley's work with education of the poor. But moreover, even if the poor were not able to educate themselves, it is the work of charity to provide for them, not government.

As discussed previously, the taking of something by force to give to another is not charity and is not condoned by the gospel of Jesus. The same applies to education services. Americans are among the most generous people in the world, and there are trillions of dollars of accumulated funds in charitable, educational, and other non-profit organizations. If education wasn't provided by expensive state monopolies, low-cost, effective schools would be affordable to most people. For those who couldn't provide, they would be able to rely on real private charity instead of government pseudo-charity that distorts the markets for education services.

32. Buy Local/Buy American/Self-Sufficiency

When your merchandise went out on the seas, you satisfied many nations; with your great wealth and your wares you enriched the kings of the earth. (Ez 27:33)

The quotation from Ezekiel above refers to the ancient city of Tyre. Its seaports and easy access made it an important center for trade, with goods from all over the world being exchanged. It became a very wealthy and powerful city through its exchange of goods from over a wide area. Ezekiel predicted the downfall of Tyre because of the pride and arrogance of the people. It parallels the warning in Proverbs that "Pride goes before destruction, a haughty spirit before a fall." (Prv 16:18)

While the message of the prophet is about the destruction of great and powerful cities that forsake God and His laws, there are important underlying realities that we can understand with an economic point of view. Interregional exchange was recognized as an important ingredient in the rise of Tyre and other significant trade centers. While the message is that the proud and the haughty can fall, a look beyond the obvious will give a picture of how and why nations develop.

As discussed in chapter 1, people do things because of the results that they expect. Their expectations are derived from experience, reading, teachers, and so on. If action A is chosen, result A is expected. If action B is chosen, result B is expected. Because of the uncertainty of the future, things might not always turn out the way they were expected to, but the choice is made based on expectations. Each person has different assumptions about reality and about what the future holds, and thus values time and other resources differently. That is what makes human society vibrant and interesting and what makes markets work. Because people value things differently, trades can be made that benefit all parties.

With every choice you make, you demonstrate your preferences in a concrete way. You decide what you want to give up in order to get something else that you want more. That is what rational decision making is all about. The idea of opportunity cost enters every decision that every person makes. The costs factored into decisions include time, monetary expenditure, physical effort, and expected enjoyment.

To some people, time is very important. They will tend to favor actions that preserve their time. Some people like doing things the easy way and take whatever results they can get. Others value aesthetics and will incur more cost to satisfy those values. All of these things are important when dealing with markets and buying and selling.

Buying local is a philosophy that has become popular. It is based on the notion that buying local is good for the buyer, good for the local economy, and good for society overall. While that may be true in some circumstances, it is worthwhile to examine the issue further to see whether it really is good from an overall perspective.

Whether or not buying local is good for the buyer depends on the assumptions and expectations of the individual. It is often possible to get some food that is fresher, better tasting, and more nutritious from local sources, though that is not necessarily the case. In order to get those benefits, however, there may be opportunity costs to consider.

A person who highly values time or convenience would likely favor a centralized market that has everything needed in a single location. There may be gourmet cooks for whom nothing but the freshest, tastiest, best-looking product will do. Such a person will likely seek separate specialty markets. There are others who like getting a good deal, and they will shop around for sales and the lowest prices. None of these choices is unreasonable, given the preferences of each person.

Similarly, if buying local is important to some people, then it makes sense for them to prefer and to seek the products that fit their preferences. They will support local producers as much as they can. The economic question is to what extent buying local helps the local or national economy.

By all means, buying from a local supplier helps that supplier. It increases demand for his products, keeps his prices up, and makes him more profitable. If, as a consumer, it gives you the overall highest satisfaction of all available choices, then all is good. If, however, you have to spend extra money for the local product, then the money that you would have saved if you bought elsewhere is no longer available to buy a shirt or a gallon of gasoline or anything else that you could do with your money. If you had to spend your time traveling to various markets with the objective of finding locally grown food, you no longer have that time available to go to a movie or your child's little league game or to make any other use of your time. There is an opportunity cost for everything.

All prosperity originates through trade. Even inherited wealth or lottery winnings first arise from someone producing something of value and trading with others. Gold nuggets that you may find in the ground would be worthless unless someone was willing to give you something of value in trade for them. The division of labor and comparative advantage make people and geographic regions more productive than they would be if they didn't specialize, as discussed in previous sections. Trading of that increased productivity with others allows each person to benefit from the productivity of those others.

Trade over a wider area enhances the benefits of the division of labor and comparative advantage because, with a greater number of people, it is likely that someone will be able to produce a good or provide a service cheaper, more efficiently or offer more value in some other way. That increased efficiency of each participant results in lower costs for each in the long run.

The lower costs from increased efficiency ultimately reduce the real cost of living, and the lower real cost of living is a benefit to all people, but especially to the poor, who have to work less hard to provide the necessities for their families. Buying local is good if it gives the most satisfaction to the buyers. It does not, however, result in improved welfare for anyone if it excludes exchanges with more efficient producers from other areas.

33. Stop Evictions Now

When a man makes a vow to the Lord or takes an oath to obligate himself by a pledge, he must not break his word but must do everything he said. (Nm 30:2)

The sight of a family being evicted is heart wrenching. People don't like to see it happen. It is natural for many to want to do something about it. There are many things that can be done by charitable people to help the families in need. Christ calls his followers to be compassionate and to help brothers and sisters when they fall on hard times.

One of the responses of many church organizations and activist groups is the pursuit of political intervention to legally block the eviction from occurring. It is a reaction that bubbles up from good intentions, but like so many other cases, those good intentions have serious negative side effects when they ignore the economic laws that rule in all human interaction. That intervention may certainly help particular families stay in their homes, but it does damage to other individuals, the economy, and to society as a whole.

Evictions can occur for a variety of reasons, including the nonpayment of rents, defaulting on mortgage contracts or any other legally binding terms of explicit or implicit agreements. In each case, however, the reason for the parties to enter into a contract in the first place is the mutual expectation of some type of gain. Without that expectation, nobody would enter into contracts. If an eviction from rented property results from the property owner not following through on contract obligations, it is very appropriate to seek legal relief. If the terms of an agreement were not formalized on paper, the terms would be generally imputed from the general practice in the locality. If there is no long-term contract for rents, for instance, the enforceable terms in many localities are typically month to month. Unless the tenant is willing to commit for a longer term, either party has the right to terminate the agreement on a month-to-month basis.

The rule of law and the strong support of agreements and contracts are key ingredients in the development of prosperous societies. When the full benefits will be realized only in the distant future, the more that people can rely on others following through on their obligations, the more likely they are to make agreements with others. The case of mortgage and loan contracts quickly comes to mind. The uncertainty of events far into the future makes people less eager to loan money for long periods of time without some additional assurance that the money will be paid back. The time value of money and the risk of uncertainty play a significant role in negotiation of long-term contracts.

A loan contract is a promise to pay back the loaned amount plus interest and fees according to agreed upon terms pertinent to the administration of the loan. A mortgage contract is the agreement to use a specific piece of property as collateral for the loan. The status of a mortgage contract is usually linked to performance of the terms of the loan.

One of the terms that a borrower specifically agrees to upon signing a mortgage contract is that, if the borrower defaults on the terms of the loan contract, the loan is payable in full and the lender can foreclose on the property. The lender has the legal right to sell the property to satisfy the balance on the loan, a right specifically acknowledged by the borrower in the mortgage contract.

The attempt to use political means to stop evictions for anything but the failure of the lender to honor terms of the contract is a proposal for the outright repudiation of the terms of the contract that was signed by all contracting parties. This may stop the impending eviction, but it demonstrates willful dishonesty on the part of the borrower, failing to live by the terms that were used to induce the lender to lend. It is, in essence, fraud. It also demonstrates total disregard for property rights by the politician.

There are many reasons why a borrower may not be able to comply with the terms of an agreement. It usually makes sense for the lender to work with the borrower to prevent foreclosure and make the best of a bad situation, and that is often the case. Banks are not in the business of owning and managing property, and they generally would prefer to collect the loan as agreed to in the contract. Even if the lender refuses to do that, however, the borrower still has an obligation that he or she committed to in good faith.

If it becomes the general case that lenders are not able to enforce mortgage contracts against higher-risk borrowers, the obvious fallout would be that the lenders would no longer offer mortgage loans to higher-risk borrowers. Inability to enforce contracts would create a moral hazard whereby the successful repudiation of contracts by people in certain conditions would encourage more people to seek those conditions, so that they could repudiate their contracts. An example might be where a political designation of "distressed neighborhood" would be a requirement for legal alteration of loan terms. In that case, there is an incentive for people to apply political pressure to have their neighborhood designated as distressed, so that they could meet the qualifying conditions. That may help those particular borrowers, but the designation as a distressed area will likely mean that it will be extremely difficult for anyone else to get a mortgage loan there. That hurts both buyers and sellers. The breakdown of contract enforceability has tremendous negative effects on any society that engages in it.

Countries that do not uphold contracts find that few contracts are entered into. All trade is based upon the expectation of performance of contract obligations, including the loaning and paying back of money. If the potential lender is very uncertain of the ability to enforce repayment, the lender will either need large down payments up front, high interest rates, or would likely find better uses for the money, uses that will offer less risk of nonpayment or will provide more current enjoyment.

It is critical to maintain the rule of law and the upholding of contracts in a free society. Contract is a foundation for developed society, but even more importantly, following through on agreements is a moral obligation that was emphasized throughout the Bible.

34. Welfare/Redistribution Programs

"Which of these three do you think was a neighbor to the man who fell into the hands of robbers?" The expert in the law replied, "the one who had mercy on him." Jesus told him, "Go and do likewise." (Lk 10:36–37)

The gospel of Jesus calls us, as Christians, to care for those who are not able to take care of themselves, the crippled, the homeless, the orphans. There are many ways to do those things, as there are many ways to accomplish everything in life. Also like everything else in life, there are effective methods and there are ineffective methods.

When using the term "welfare," it is important to realize that the hundreds of government programs justified by that term don't all translate into helping the poor. Government programs can be better understood as falling into two different categories: 1) welfare for the not-poor, often described as corporate welfare, and 2) welfare for the poor.

In both categories, redistribution takes center stage. Redistribution is taking property from one person to give to another, based on the ideas of someone in power regarding justice or rightness or fairness. The concept of redistribution, however, is necessarily based on the violation of the Commandments. It is the use of force for the involuntary transfer of wealth from individuals to the government. That the aim of the government agency is to give it to others is not a justification for the confiscation.

The first category, corporate welfare, is pretty clear-cut in its implications. It is basically the taking of money from ordinary citizens, including the poor, and giving it to well-connected businesses and, very often, to the wealthy people who own them. Corporate welfare takes many forms and manifests itself in a myriad of government programs. Many of these programs use the excuse that they will stimulate the economy, and thus help society in general. The fallacy behind all of these programs is that, in order for the government to give money to an individual or business to stimulate economic activity, it must take it from other people. Those other people no longer have the money to invest in their own projects, their own businesses, or to stimulate the economy by spending it on items of their own choosing.

A quick example may make it clearer. Let's imagine economic "stimulation" by a private individual. Say a businessman employs 100 people. He decides to do some economic development. By doubling the size of his business, he could hire 100 more people. That would be a boon for the local population, but it would be very expensive. He uses that to rationalize the idea of sending armed thugs out to collect money from each family in the area, since they would all benefit. That would be too much of a burden on the limited number of local people, however, so he decides to send them to collect from everyone in the entire region. Since each person would only be out a small amount, they would hardly have anything to complain about; and look at what good it would do for the local people.

Obviously, the employer stealing from residents is wrong, whether or not 100 people are hired or the local economy is stimulated. The employer gains, the new employees gain, and maybe even a number of other local people gain. The money taken from others, however, is no longer available for them to do with it whatever else they might have done to stimulate the economy however they chose to.

When a politician does the same thing under the guise of economic development or stimulus, it is no less theft. It is no less benefiting some at the expense of others. An honorable, charitable person, whether he or she is a politician or a lesser being, does not steal, either for himself or for anyone else.

The stimulus and development programs are all another example of the broken-window fallacy, only looking at what is seen here and now and ignoring all of the very important, but unseen, effects that may accumulate for other people and in the future. A million-dollar economic development project may indeed spur business, cause the hiring of employees, and improve the condition of some specific, identifiable people. That is what is seen. What is not seen is that those who pay for it must involuntarily sacrifice their own well being for the sake of those who become wealthy from the development projects.

Direct subsidies, price supports, import tariffs, market restrictions, and dozens of variations all take money from one party to make another not-poor party better off. They have no moral imperative and, in sum, constitute welfare for the wealthy.

The next category is by far the more important one for Christians, because it seems to follow from what many interpret Jesus' words to mean. It includes helping the hungry, the naked, the homeless, the thirsty, and the stranger. A look at the parable of the Good Samaritan is very enlightening as to what Jesus meant when he called his disciples to charity.

A man was beaten, robbed, and left in the ditch on the side of the road to die. A priest and a Levite, both of the elite class of Jesus' day, walked by and ignored him, leaving him to suffer and die. A Samaritan, one of the lowly, despised class at whom the priests and Levites looked down their noses, saw the man and had mercy. He took him to an inn, made sure that he was taken care of, and paid for his care out of his own pocket. The point of the parable is obvious, that only the Samaritan was charitable.

Imagine the same story now, with a man, beaten, robbed, and dying in a ditch. This time, the priest decides to do something.

When he sees the Levite coming, he lets him pass by. When he sees the Samaritan man coming, he puts a sword to his throat and forces him to pay for the care of the injured man. Did the Samaritan act out of mercy? Did the priest do what Jesus was commanding? Obviously they did not. Jesus never, ever, in any of his teachings promoted the idea of using force or stealing from someone else to do one's charity. The idea is absurd. That is not charity at all.

Jesus' program (the first scenario) is Christian charity. The second scenario is government welfare programs. Arrogant politicians pretend to be charitable with money they steal from others, while their own wealth is cleverly squirreled away in protective trusts, foundations, and favored corporations.

A further implication of forced charity is that it displaces true charity. People who are forced to give to government for welfare are much less compelled by conscience to promote private charity. In the Gospel of Mark, Chapter 7, Jesus discussed the Jews' concept of "Corban." Instead of obeying the commandment to honor their fathers and mothers, he told them: "You say that if a man says to his father or mother: 'Whatever help you might otherwise have received from me is Corban' (that is, a gift devoted to God), then you no longer let him do anything for his father or mother. Thus you nullify the word of God by your own tradition that you have handed down."

The point that Jesus made is that, no matter what rules the authorities make, nobody is released from responsibility to care for his or her family, young or old. He also repeatedly reminded his disciples that true charity meant that they had a responsibility to help those who were prevented from being productive by physical limitations, who had no way of adequately providing for themselves.

In the parable of the talents, Jesus called all who are capable of being productive to do so. (Mt 25:14–30) A talent was a very large amount of money, but it can also be a metaphor for the skills and abilities that we call talents in the present day. Whether you are given ten talents or one talent, you are called to use them or it productively. That productivity is the only thing that charitable people can use for their charity. People are called to provide for themselves and their families if they are able to. Those who are not able to do that must rely on charity. Charity is the job of the church and charitable people.

With that said, it is obvious that many people have come to depend on the government for support and would have a difficult time if that support was suddenly removed. Of any program of government, welfare for truly poor and starving individuals at least has as its goal trying to help those in need. The ultimate aim of any type of welfare program must be to increase the skills and independence of the individuals. Any program that makes people dependent is not only immoral, it also doesn't meet the criteria of helping the poor in the long run.

The decades long "War on Poverty" has squandered trillions of dollars of taxpayer money, but there is no less poverty today than there was when it started. There is only a complex maze of massive government bureaucracies. The program is a failure because the good intentions are backed up by violation of the rights of individuals and distortions of economic incentives.

Proverbs 24:33–34 gives the reason that the programs increase poverty rather than decrease it: "A little sleep, a little slumber, a little folding of the hands to rest—and poverty will come on you like a bandit and scarcity like an armed man." The inverse of that idea is given in Proverbs 16:26: "The laborer's appetite works for him; his hunger drives him on." People are productive when there is incentive to work.

The people who are truly without means for survival are a very small portion of the total population in any developed society. They are definitely dependent on others for their well-being, but in total, they would not be a very great burden for charitable givers. The wife of noble character in Proverbs 31 "opens her arms to the poor and extends her hands to the needy," because she is productive and has resources to be charitable. The more of her resources that are taken in taxes, the less resources she has for her charity. The more that is provided by government programs, the less incentive for truly charitable people to be charitable. It is a cycle of perverse incentives.

Helping the poor includes giving them responsibility for their own lives and allowing the incentives of society to drive them to be productive and improve their skills, all ideas that have their foundations in biblical wisdom and have been understood for thousands of years. Every society at any time will have some people who are not capable of taking care of themselves, and it is the job of Christians to take care of them. The highest level of achievement in aiding the poor with Christian dignity, however, is to help a person get to the point where he can help others.

35. Socialized Medicine/ Universal Health Care

And he said to them: "You have a fine way of setting aside the commands of God in order to observe your own traditions!" (Mk 7:9)

Health-care markets are not at all difficult to describe or understand. Health care is a service provided by one person to someone else. That is it's essence. Each of the millions of separate transactions on the markets each day arises from and results in the prices we see for those services. While the interactions of the millions of individuals are incredibly complex, the economic laws and the system of cause-and-effect relationships are not complex and are easily understood.

The difficulties we are witnessing in health-care markets are the result of the arrogance of central planners acting on the "pretense of knowledge," so eloquently described by Friedrich August von Hayek (1899–1992). Central planning of an economy, or in this case, of the health-care industry, is an impossible task and is doomed to failure at the outset. It is obvious that the more deeply involved that centralized government planners worm their way into the markets, the more dislocated and less effective the market gets. The last few decades have seen a tremendous rise in government regulation and manipulation of health-care markets, and, simultaneously, the problems have multiplied.

It is important to be healthy, but having health care is no more important than having food to eat. The market forces that govern the prices, supply, and demand for potatoes and spaghetti are the same forces that govern the prices, supply, and demand for pediatric visits and heart surgeries.

It has become an unquestioned assumption that everyone deserves Mercedes Benz medical care, even if they have a Tata[38] budget. Of course, it would be nice for everyone to be able to afford Mercedes Benz care, just as it would be nice for everyone to be able to afford filet mignon at five-star restaurants every night. The economic reality is that people are different, they earn different levels of income, and can afford different levels of health care.

The implication with universal, government-provided health care is that everyone has a right to the best care, no matter what his or her financial circumstances. That is, however, equivalent to insisting that all people have a right to the best food, whether they can afford it or not. The reality is that it ends up being neither the best food nor the best medical care. Central planners make the choices and necessarily limit who gets care and what level of care they get. It is typical of central planning that the elite political group gets top-notch services, the rest get what they are told they are allowed to have.

As with all economic phenomena, we must clearly understand that charitable intentions do not suspend the laws of economics. These laws prevail whether intentions are good, bad, or indifferent. Market exchange is the transfer of something of value between two parties who prefer what the other person has more than they prefer the things that they themselves have. It is the basis for the creation of value in society and the source of income and wealth, which in turn allows people to be charitable. The results of the exchanges are governed by economic law, as falling objects are governed by gravity.

Charity means voluntarily providing for others from your own

---

[38] Tata is an Indian brand of car, with the cheapest model, The Nano, starting at $2,200, including taxes and dealer fees.

accumulated wealth, your time, and your energy [as with Mother Theresa bathing lepers] out of the goodness of your heart. It is a very important part of the Christian life, and Christians are called to be charitable. The Christian is never called, however, to pick his neighbor's pocket to provide charity.

Government provision of health care, or any benefit for that matter, involves the involuntary taking from one person to give to another. That is not charity at all, but rather coercion and theft. The parable of the Good Samaritan (Lk 10:30–37) is especially appropriate here. The man who was beaten and left to die was in critical need of health care. The Samaritan did not leave his care to the priests, Pharisees, or any other government official of his time. He used his own resources for his own charity. He brought him to the inn and paid for his care.

It may be said that, because the cost of health care is increasing so rapidly, it is not possible for private charity to take care of the health needs of the poor. A few questions arise from that view: If a society with a given, limited set of resources cannot possibly provide health care through private, voluntary methods, why would that same society, with the same limited resources, magically be able to provide those same services through government, with its extra overhead, when the government gets its resources only from the people of the society? Furthermore, why is it that the cost of health care has been increasing so rapidly in the decades since government has gotten involved? Whether it is provided by government, by private organizations, or by individuals, health care will still ultimately come from the resources of the people. There is no other source. Prices of health care inflate so rapidly because government programs inject hundreds of billions of dollars into the industry. Those dollars have to come from somewhere, however. The rest of the economy suffers as fewer dollars are available for other goods or services.

In a free market, where all transactions are voluntary, the

natural, undeniable, long-term tendency in all cases, all throughout the history of society, is for real, inflation-adjusted prices to decrease. In agricultural production, real prices have decreased to a tiny fraction of what they were a century or a millennium ago. It now takes a relatively short time working to provide adequate food, even as fewer and fewer farmers are needed. They would be even lower absent the interference of politics in agriculture. Efficiency in agriculture causes prices to decrease, except in those instances where government intervention keeps them high.

A more striking example can be seen in the market for any new technology. Computers typically double in capacity and functionality every 18 months. Meanwhile, the prices keep dropping. It is now possible to have, on a tiny portable computer, more computing power and more memory than a skyscraper full of computing equipment of a few short decades ago, and at a tiny fraction of the price.

An interesting characteristic of modern medical services is that a large part of them is based on technology. As with any other case in voluntary markets, the prices of the technology and services involved in medical care should be drastically decreasing over time as the markets become more efficient. The reality is that medical care is not a free, voluntary market at all. Government seriously intervenes at all stages, in nearly all services.

Massive amounts of money and resources are diverted by government from the voluntary market and are injected into health-care markets. At least 45% of medical costs are now paid for by government, with the proportion increasing over time. A significant portion of payments by insurance companies is mandated by government, payments that add to the money being pumped into the system, distorting the markets.

The injected money artificially stimulates demand for medical services, many of which would not be utilized if the individual had to pay for them. This excess demand tends to raise prices. The high prices and corresponding profits give incentives for health-care suppliers to develop new, more expensive equipment and treatments. The higher prices themselves justify further injections of money, taken by government from other markets. It is a self-reinforcing cycle where medical prices are inflated at the expense of all voluntary markets. The intervention distorts the price signals to the market participants and the inflation in prices is focused where the most money is injected.

The major difficulty with understanding health care, as with most other major problems in society, is the tendency of economic planners to lump things into aggregates. Health care is viewed as a homogeneous reservoir that people can tap into whenever they have a need. The reality of health care is that there is a vast selection of different goods and services, each with its separate supply, demand, and price. Individuals are no longer responsible for the bulk of their medical cost. They have little incentive to choose what they can afford, which would keep prices down, because most of the cost is paid for by someone else.

There is also a large array of health problems, which can each be treated at different levels of care and with alternate methods. For many typical problems, a medical doctor is not needed. A practitioner with a fairly low level of training and a consequent low cost could be used to treat those cases. Government-sponsored or - sanctioned monopolies in various areas of health care, however, keep low-cost providers out and allow premium providers to enjoy monopoly or near-monopoly prices.

In summary, the problems that are plaguing the health-care markets are not problems of the markets at all. They are the results of government central planning and interference in the markets. The injections of money inflate prices, the removal of personal responsibility increases demand for less-efficient solutions, and the exclusion of effective competition enables the entrenched providers to charge higher prices than they would be able to with truly voluntary markets. As in all cases, central planning will lead to the ultimate breakdown of markets. Central planning and markets are not compatible, in health care or any other area of human society.

In order to avoid the problems of central planning in health care, it is necessary to remove the central planner and place the planning and responsibility back with the individual health-care consumers and providers. The problems of providing for the needs of the truly needy will then be minimized, and true Christian charity will then be able to take back its proper role from the purveyors of false charity and destructive manipulation of markets.

36. Insurance Regulations

The prudent see danger and take refuge, but the simple keep going and suffer for it. (Prv 27:12)

As with health care and all other markets, the basics of insurance are not really that complex and difficult to understand. The difficulties come from the politics introduced by central planners who operate with the false notion that they can know more than the market can.

In a free market, insurance serves a very valuable purpose. It is the pooling of risk among members of a large group of people or organizations. It is used for protecting individual members of the pool against the devastating effects of large losses. Every person is able to shoulder a portion of the cost over a period of time, but the burden of the full cost of the insured event at one time would mean possible bankruptcy. The participants in the insurance plan pay a portion of the cost of an insured event in return for having the insurance pool pay for the loss when and if it occurs.

Insurance works because the risk is divided among the participants. Those with higher risks carry a higher cost of insurance. A more expensive home will require a higher premium than a lower-priced home, because the expected loss is probably going to be greater when a covered event happens.

In order for insurance to work, it must meet a couple of important requirements. The risk must be random, and the covered event must be relatively rare. While the total number of occurrences can be estimated fairly accurately for the group in the coming time period covered by the policy, the individuals that will incur the loss cannot be known or knowable. On the other hand, if 100% of the participants will incur the insured event in the covered period, it makes no sense to incur the extra administrative costs of a third-party insurer. In that case, the administrative costs will make the premiums paid in more than each participant would have paid had they covered the cost on their own.

Take the case of home owner's insurance. In a given group of policy holders, 1 in 500 may have a fire every year. Nobody in the group knows, however, whose house will be the one to burn. Each policy holder shares the cost, but only the fire victim gets the benefit. A homeowner who set his own house on fire is specifically excluded from receiving benefits, because it is not a random event. Policy holders can control whether they set a fire. It is uninsurable.

Another uninsurable event is one that happens before the policy is effective. If a house burns down and then the owner buys insurance on it, he can't expect the policy to pay for the prior fire. In that case, it is not random. The probability of a loss is 100%. It is already done. Insurance policies specifically exclude prior events.

A free-market in insurance would offer consumers the choice of how to address their risk. Some may choose to save the money on premiums and pay for the losses when they occur. In that case the consumer is self-insuring. Insurance companies have to pay salaries, costs, and dividends to investors, but they also have a large amount of money that they can efficiently invest, which can help reduce premiums. The market for insurance policies will determine the price, and the price will determine whether the consumer finds it more beneficial to self-insure or to share the risk with a pool of similar people.

Health insurance is a special case because a significant portion of the cost now included in health-insurance premiums cannot, in any coherent sense, be considered insurance at all. Only a portion of health premiums actually serve the real purpose of pooling the risk of catastrophic illness or injury.

Instead of remaining strictly insurance, the policies have become a type of prepaid medical plan in addition to insuring against loss. Because many medical plans are provided through the employer and enjoy favored tax status, there has been overwhelming pressure to include every conceivable type of expense related to health care in the policy in order to maximize the pre-tax nature of the payments.

A routine visit to the doctor or dentist is not, in any way, an insurable event. The patient makes a conscious choice to incur the cost. The amount of the charge is not large, and thus will not break the family bank if they paid it. It is an event that most people will endure on a regular basis, whether or not an insurance policy is in place.

We can again use the home insurance as an analogy. It is easier to understand because government mandates have not distorted it to nearly the extent they have with health insurance. Imagine, if you will, that all homeowners' insurance policies included things like painting, roofing, siding, bathroom repairs, smoke alarms, and so on. They are all valid expenses, all items for which individual home owners are willing to pay.

When the insurance policy covers them, policy holders will paint their houses more often, install nicer bathroom fixtures, use ceramic tile in the kitchen instead of vinyl, and so on. They will use more of the expensive insured services because they are free. It is the moral-hazard phenomenon again. The incentives built into the system will result in rapid expansion of the use of the supposedly free stuff.

The problem for everyone in the plan is that none of the stuff is really free. The more expensive the repairs, the higher the premiums that must be charged to cover them. The incentive is to abuse the others in the plan to get better stuff than you would have gotten had you paid for it yourself. It would be a moral hazard to require a homeowners insurance policy to cover uninsurable events.

Fortunately for homeowners, that has not yet happened and homeowners insurance is still affordable.

That is not the case for medical insurance. Every state has a list of mandated coverage for the plans offered in the state. Under federal rules, minimum coverage of a multitude of uninsurable events is required in order to qualify as an acceptable plan. In all, hundreds of mandated items are included, even though most people would not pay the extra for the coverage if they had the choice. Plans are generally required to cover every person for the same premium, no matter what the risk.

Many people would be willing to pay for a bare-bones policy that offered just the coverage they wanted and needed. That policy would offer quite low premiums and shoulder only the risk of catastrophic illness. The charge against the idea for many people is that offering this program would exclude high-risk participants from low-cost programs. Being pooled with other high risks, they would be forced to pay higher premiums or may not be able to get insurance at all.

It is true that some people would have to pay higher premiums. But in any case, forcing other people to pay higher insurance premiums even though they don't want and need them is not insurance. It is redistribution. It is taking money from one person, in the form of higher premiums than they otherwise would pay, and giving it to the other in the form of lower premiums than they would otherwise pay. It is neither fair nor right. To the extent that the premiums are higher for the low-risk policy holder, it is coerced charity to the high-risk participant, which only tends to confuse the insurance issue and corrupt the decision-making process for all participants. Redistribution is not insurance, and forcing it onto insurance consumers has negative consequences for all involved.

For true insurance, only those with similar risks can be pooled together. A professional stunt man chooses a career that is much more dangerous than a checkout register clerk or a radio announcer.

It can rightly be expected that the medical expenses for the stunt man would be thousands of dollars higher than those for the clerk or announcer on a year-in and year-out basis. In most plans, however, the clerk-type person must pay higher premiums to cover the cost of the stunt-man risks. Had the stunt man and the clerk been in separate pools, the clerk would have paid premiums commensurate with the risk associated with the activities. The stunt man would and should have paid much higher premiums commensurate with the higher expected medical bills.

Insurance, at its base, is nothing more than a service that a company provides to help mitigate risk for the policy holders. In a free, voluntary market, the needs of the insurance provider would be balanced against the desires of the consumer. Those companies that did not offer competitive service would lose out to others that offered better service. Companies that consistently abused customers would soon have none.

A significant problem with the current health-insurance situation is that it is intimately tied to the health-care-provision industry. Premiums are so high that many people, especially the poor, cannot afford them. As far as providing health care for the poor is concerned, that has nothing to do with insurance. It is charity, pure and simple. Including the issue of poverty and charity in health care and insurance is an unnecessary confusion that does not help, but rather makes it worse.

Of course, we as Christians should care for the poor. We are called to be compassionate, to follow the example of the Good Samaritan. There are thousands of charitable, nonprofit organizations and trusts with cumulative assets of trillions of dollars. The health care of the poor is an appropriate target for them to use their money. Specialty organizations, such as the various cancer, AIDS, and multiple-sclerosis societies are in an ideal position to provide for the care of those with the diseases who cannot afford treatment.

The current state of affairs is that there is no free and voluntary market in insurance, especially with regard to health insurance. The premiums for health-care insurance are high because they include many costs that are not truly insurance costs. They include uninsurable events and charity, and they pool risks that are inappropriate to pool. The costs are spiraling up because the system inherently rewards overuse and inflated prices for new medical techniques.

Government meddling in the insurance industry is the primary cause for the dislocation and rapidly-rising prices. The solution is to reduce the influence of government on market decisions and ultimately to limit it to making sure that contractual obligations of all parties are followed, in the tradition of justice outlined in the Ten Commandments.

37. International Development Programs

Each man should give what he has decided in his heart to give, not reluctantly or under compulsion, for God loves a cheerful giver. (2 Cor 9:7)

God loves a cheerful giver, and the gospel of Christ calls us to be charitable. God does not, however, call us to compel others to give according to what we think is appropriate.

International-aid programs are government entities that get their money from compulsion. The primary fact is that using the force of government to take from one person or group involuntarily to give to another is theft. It is breaking the commandments, and is thus not an appropriate channel for Christians to propose for their charity, whether domestically or internationally.

The secondary but extremely important issue is that, whether or not it is morally right, it is practically counterproductive. The reality of aid programs is that they ignore the source of poverty in the target country,

The late Peter Bauer was an economist who specialized in development economics when it was beginning to flourish, and he spent a great deal of time and effort studying and writing about the conditions in third-world countries and the policies of the governments of the developed world. According to Bauer, "The primary result of official Western aid has been the creation of the Third World as a collectivity confronting the West, and one that, as a collectivity, is hostile to it. The second major consequence has been the politicization of life in the Third World."[39] He goes on to say, "The frequency and intensity of the internal conflict in these countries is often the result of the politicization of life in the Third World. This politicization has greatly raised the stakes in the battle for power."[40]

While his work and writings emerged several decades ago, life in Third World countries is still politicized by the same process. Governments from developed countries transfer money taken from their own citizens to the governments of countries with the status of "less developed."

He described aid to the governments of countries with brutal dictators, who suppress private activity, deprive citizens of rights, and cause tremendous economic disasters. While some of the names of the dictators have changed and various other countries have joined the list, the situation remains basically the same now.

The people in Zimbabwe are starving today primarily because the government expropriated farms from the white owners and handed them out to supporters of the violent politicians. They have devolved from being the "bread basket of Africa" to Africa's biggest basket case. They have become one of the least economically free societies in the world. The inflation rate of the currency was in the multi-million percent-per-year range before the currency was suspended in 2009, in favor of foreign, more stable currencies. Whether or not the redistribution was justified or the claims of the dictator, Robert Mugabe, were true, the destruction of property rights has economic consequences.

Socialist governments, strong-arm dictators, and oppressed people characterize many countries of the Third World. They are generally among the lowest-ranking countries in the various indexes of freedom compiled from international data.

---

[39] P. T. Bauer, *Equality, The Third World, and Economic Delusion,* (Cambridge, Massachusetts: Harvard University Press, 1981), 86.

[40] P. T. Bauer, *Equality,* 89.

If Christians and other people are truly interested in the development of poor countries and the welfare of the people who live in them, then the cause of the poverty must be addressed and eradicated first. The oppression by their own governments and deep-seated corruption prevent any sort of development. Lack of property rights and institutions to protect them will ensure that the poor never accumulate any significant wealth.

The conditions in those countries are reminiscent of those described in Proverbs and Ecclesiastes: "A poor man's field may produce abundant food, but injustice sweeps it away." (Prv 13:23) "If you see the poor oppressed in a district, and justice and rights denied, do not be surprised by such things; for one official is eyed by a higher one, and over them both are others higher still. The increase of the land is taken by all; the king himself profits from the fields." (Eccl 5:8–9)

People are poor because of injustice, and the injustice arises from their own government. Without addressing the root cause, the resulting conditions will never change. Much of the money sent to the corrupt politicians and wasteful socialist bureaucracies will be squandered. It will be spent on the Three Ms of development, as described by Bauer: monuments, Mercedes, and machine guns.

Rather than lifting countries out of poverty, the system entrenches it. As is the case with every problem, throwing money at it doesn't make it go away, even if the money is thrown with good intentions. Unfortunately, a massive worldwide development bureaucracy has grown up around the program. Mercedes Benz–driving development experts get wealthy dispensing money to their wards, as hundreds of billions of dollars of free money flow through the pipelines. There is little incentive for the development experts to encourage the conditions that would actually bring about development. Their cushy jobs depend on continuing impoverishment of the Third World countries dependent on the system.

The system is broken, the incentives are backward, and nobody is accountable. The root cause of the political strife and resulting economic breakdown is the system of foreign aid as it has existed for decades. Trillions of dollars of aid that have been funneled into these countries have been wasted. It hasn't worked because it can't work.

The system itself is based on socialist central planning at all levels. Whether or not there are sincere politicians in the poor countries, central planning, as we have said so many times, will prevent progress. Its foundation is fallacy, its methods are based on arrogance and condescension.

Professor William Easterly is the contemporary heir to the mantle passed on by Peter Bauer. His books, *Tyranny of Experts*, *The White Man's Burden*, and others, as well as his numerous speeches and other publications, have done a lot to shed light on many of the human rights disasters being promoted as international development and foreign aid.

There will likely be little progress in many less-developed countries until the prevailing foreign aid apparatus is dismantled and the corruption ended. As Christians, we need to be involved on the ground in poor countries, as many are. But we also need to get it right when discussing development programs. In this case, good intentions not only don't help, they also severely hurt the ability of people in poor regions to lift themselves from poverty and attain dignity by fighting for economic freedom and property rights.

38. Kyoto Protocol/ Global Warming Legislation

Woe to those who plan iniquity, to those who plot evil on their beds. At morning's light they carry it out because it is in their power to do it. They covet fields and seize them, and houses, and take them. They defraud a man of his home, a fellowman of his inheritance. (Mi 2:1–2)

Global warming has been a pivotal issue on the political scene for some time now. Many fear that the earth's temperature is rising due to an increase in carbon dioxide and other hydrocarbons in the atmosphere from anthropogenic, or manmade, sources. The escalating carbon dioxide is blamed solely on developed societies and their the burning of fossil fuels to power industrialization. The Kyoto Protocol is an international agreement, supposedly binding on all signatories, to drastically reduce carbon dioxide emissions.

There is a trade-off in the choices to be made with regard to reducing CO_2 emissions. Industrialization brings with it an increased standard of living for everyone in those societies that engage in it, including the poor. It is quite obvious to anyone who cares to notice that the poor in developed countries are many times better off than the poor in destitute, undeveloped countries. A reduction in the emissions to the levels prescribed in the Protocol would require drastic deindustrialization of the nations so subjected. That would have the greatest effect on the poor, as fewer profits and less income means less left over for charitable giving.

The other side of the coin is the fear that continuing on the current path will lead to massive environmental catastrophes and

175

social upheaval. The science on the issue is far from settled, however, with thousands scientists worldwide signing a petition against the Kyoto Protocol. Many have defected from the so-called consensus because of what they see as politicization of the science. While many agree that the temperature is indeed increasing, it is such a slow rate that it will not have the tremendous impact that others say it will. Others see alternate causes and anticipate a possible reversal toward global cooling, as it has in all previous cycles. In any case, those scientists believe that the difference in temperature achieved by meeting the goals of the protocol will be minor and not worth the tremendous burden of economic costs.

Whether or not the trend will be warming or cooling in the future, whether or not it is manmade, and whether or not there will be disastrous consequences, all of the proposed solutions involve central planning of a few self-anointed "wise men." As with all forms of centralized planning authority, it is bound to produce perverse results and bring misery to everyone on whom it gets its tentacles.

The global-warming movement is about power, not about the planet, not about people, not about humanitarianism. It is another more deceptive face of socialist central planning. The powers behind the movement are very wealthy politicians who have positioned themselves to profit handsomely from the scare mongering and political upheaval they are inducing. As the verse from Micah said: ". . . they carry it out because it is in their power to do it. They covet fields and seize them, and houses and take them. They defraud a man of his home, a fellowman of his inheritance." They use the power of government for their own profit. Corruption is reigning in the politics of global warming because people are getting very rich and powerful by manipulating public opinion and the public purse.

Even with the best of intentions, central planners could not possibly know what will happen in the future. The computer models that they use cannot even accurately predict what has already happened in the past. Every model must use data to drive the results. The millions of sources of inputs that affect the real climate would make any model so complex as to be worthless. Simplifications are made to make it workable, but those simplifications make them unrealistic and untruthful.

Even if it was possible to take into account all of the possible variables that affect the global climate, it is not possible to know what events will occur in the future to provide those inputs. The changes in the sun's radiation, shifting continents and ocean currents, devastating volcanic eruptions, and so on are all unpredictable and unavoidable. The best models cannot possibly predict the future climate because the future inputs to the system cannot be known.

The best that human society will be able to do is to remain flexible to take advantage of innovation in the face of future problems. The climate has changed in cycles over millions of years. Sea levels have been rising at various rates since the end of the last glacial maximum 10,000 to 12,000 years ago. It is estimated that, at the end of the last glacial maximum, the sea level was more than 400 feet below where it is now.

Sea levels will rise, as they have since the first civilizations thousands of years ago. They will continue to rise until the earth begins the next cycle of glacial buildup, at which time they will recede. Climatic conditions will change, as they have throughout the history of the world. The earth is not stable. It is dynamic and constantly changing. Those who believe that the conditions we have now are the right conditions have no perspective on history. They are extremely unrealistic in their expectations and shallow in their understanding.

Christians believe that God is the author of life, that he is the ruler of nature, and that mankind will prosper by following God's laws. God made a wonderful universe. We find ourselves on this planet, subject to God's laws and in awe at the amazing order. We have moved from the state of destitution and poverty because individuals voluntarily interact with one another. Population is rapidly increasing in poor countries because people are living longer, are better nourished, and healthier. We use our human intelligence and ingenuity to solve the problems presented to the human race. We are productive, and build value and wealth for ourselves and others when we trade our productivity with them.

An important part of solving the problems of destitution and developing into a prosperous world is the use of energy in innovative applications. Bending the people to the will of the state planners stifles innovation and removes from the table many very effective solutions to the problems of poverty and the development of people. H. B. Phillips, quoted in F. A. Hayek's *The Constitution of Liberty*, reflected on this very situation many years ago. "... In advancing society, any restriction on liberty reduces the number of things tried and so reduces the rate of progress. In such a society freedom of action is granted to the individual, not because it gives him greater satisfaction but because if allowed to go his own way he will on average serve the rest of us better than under any orders we know how to give."

It is arrogance for powerful rulers to think that they understand all of nature and hold the key to the future. They think they have the right to subject their fellow men and women to the arbitrary rules that they make up, contrary to the laws of God. They don't have that right and they, as well as the people they manipulate, will suffer the long-term consequences of their folly.

39. Money and Inflation

You trample the poor and force him to give you grain. Therefore, though you have built stone mansions, you will not live in them; though you have lush vineyards you will not drink their wine. For I know how many are your offenses and how great your sins. You oppress the righteous and take bribes and you deprive the poor of justice in the courts. (Am 5:11)

In part 1, money was recognized as a critical component in developed societies. It is a commodity that allows for the convenient transfer of value from one person to another. It enhances trade and allows individuals to benefit from the division of labor and comparative advantage. It is a phenomenon that arises spontaneously in any society that advances beyond a primitive barter system.

While the current monetary system functions similarly to that which arises naturally from a market system, it has some major differences. Modern money is made of coins and bills of various denominations, but, much more importantly, it is made up of deposits in banks. Checking and savings accounts are a very convenient way to store value and safely pay debts.

The central banks of the United States and of many other countries can create new money through buying debt securities with only accounting entries and no underlying physical assets. Fractional reserve banks create new money when they lend out money deposited by their customers. The borrowed money is re-deposited in bank accounts and becomes new money, equivalent to and in addition to the original deposit. The central bank combines with fractional-reserve banking to create a very flexible supply of money. The idea that money can be made out of thin air, with nothing but an accounting entry is difficult to fathom, but understanding the process is a key to getting a grip on one of the greatest factors in the distortion of any economy.

Banks are required to keep on hand only a small fraction of the money that customers deposit with them, and they can lend the excess to others. The original depositor has a right to 100% access to 100% of the money in the account at all times, yet, once the excess reserves are lent out and deposited into another account, the new depositor has 100% access to 100% of the money borrowed. That means that, as soon as the loan is made from fractional reserves, new money has been made, of which multiple people have 100% ownership of the same monetary base. In this way, the money supply is multiplied many times the new reserves made available by the central bank.

It might help to go through a numerical example to see how the creation of fractional-reserve-bank money works. Say you deposit $1,000 and the reserve requirement is 10%. The bank can lend me $900 of your money and only keep $100 on hand. Once it is in my account, that $900 is my money to do with as I please. That money is also still yours. The bank owes you that money too. Instead of $1,000 of real money, there is now $1,900 of real money that you and I together can use for whatever purposes we choose. In effect, $900 was created out of thin air. Pretty amazing. This is multiplied, as 90% of my deposit can be lent out, and so on down the line. Ultimately, a 10% reserve requirement can expand the money supply 10 times the original deposit.

The result of constantly increasing the money supply is a decrease in the value of all of the dollars that existed before the new money entered the system. It is similar to a pitcher of lemonade. The addition of extra water dilutes the existing lemonade. As the dollar is devalued, or diluted through inflation, it takes more dollars to buy a given set of goods and the price of everything that is bought and sold increases.

The value of the dollar in 1913 was approximately equal to what it was more than 100 years prior to that, at the founding of this country. In 1913, Congress established the central bank of the United States, the Federal Reserve Bank. It assumed the role of making money, and was charged with the tasks of stabilizing the value of the dollar and preventing economic crises.

Since the founding of the Federal Reserve Bank, rather than stabilizing the value of the dollar, it has systematically devalued it, so that it is now worth approximately 4 percent of what it was worth 100 years ago. That means that something that would cost $1 in 1913 now costs about $24.07 (October 2015), not because it is more valuable now, but only because the dollar has been diluted and devalued to less than $1/24^{th}$ of its prior value. Wealth has been transferred from consumers to the government and associated bankers, who got real lemonade and paid for it with water.

Governing authorities have used devaluation of the currency for millennia as a method of taking money from the citizens without having to use an overt tax, which tends to be unpopular. It was an important contributing factor in the fall of the Roman Empire. Currency debasement is, in effect, a stealth tax, and most modern governments deploy it on a regular basis.

Given that the second purpose of the Federal Reserve Bank was to stabilize the economy and prevent economic crises, we can see that the Fed has failed miserably in this regard also. There are regular massive economic disturbances caused by manipulation of the flexible money supply.

Given the fact that the money supply is easily and readily increased by modern monetary authorities with no necessary increase in the real value of individual goods, those authorities are directly responsible for the increase in the overall prices of goods. As various economists and central bankers have noted over the years, inflation is always and everywhere a monetary phenomenon.

Unfortunately for the citizens, the monopoly in the supply of money gives the government the ability to abuse their power in manipulating markets for political purposes. Much of the dislocation in modern society arises from that abuse. The problems with a flexible money supply, and the economic instability it induces, are not caused by money in and of itself, nor the markets of which it is such a key component. They are caused by government policy regarding money.

The important fact for this discussion is that modern society could not exist without money. It is the necessary intermediary that allows all people to benefit from trade, from the division of labor, and from comparative advantage between individuals, nations, and regions. Many people, organizations, and governments treat monetary manipulation not only as a prerogative of the government, but even as a responsibility. That treatment is based on deep-seated fallacies about money and inflation. As with so many policy issues, it rests on the false premise that government central planners can know what is best for the people, that they can know how to fix the things that are wrong, and more so that they are all honest, diligent leaders with only the best interests of their citizens in mind. It can readily be seen from history that none of those premises are true. While money is critically important in advanced society, it is important to recognize that, because it is so important, it is the most highly politicized of all commodities.

Monetary policy has transferred a tremendous amount of wealth from the poor and middle class to the wealthy, to investment bankers with connections, and to the government. They force the poor and everyone else to "give them grain," as the reference to Amos states, by devaluing the money and by creating instability in the economy. Those who promote the actions of the money manipulators also bear responsibility for the results.

As Christians we must realize the damage and the danger

arising from money manipulation. Central planners in the banking and money-creation industries need to be held accountable for what they are doing, and knowledgeable people can help to bring about that accountability.

40. How Can I Make A Difference

Then the LORD said to Moses, "Go to Pharaoh and say to him, 'This is what the LORD, the God of the Hebrews, says: Let my people go, so that they may worship me.'" (Ex 9:1)

One of the most discouraging aspects of modern defects in society is that there is nothing new under the sun. Mankind has gone through all of the problems before, many times. One would think that, eventually, an intelligent species like human beings would be able to take the important lessons from generations past and not make the same errors. That same realization, however, can also be a source of hope. We can relate to the gospel of Jesus because the human race has not changed. People are the same now as they always have been, with all of the weaknesses, strengths, negative emotions, hopes, and dreams.

The world has a lot of poor people, disease, and hunger. There is, however, less of it now than there was in prior eras. The norm for the average person throughout much of history was poverty, struggle, and short life spans. The explosion in population that we are witnessing in these times is a tribute to the increase in well being of the average person of the world. It has been noted by some development experts that people did not suddenly start breeding like rabbits; they just stopped dropping like flies. Nutrition, hygiene, technology, and health care are much better than they were, and people are living much longer than ever before, on average. As societies develop, parents have fewer children because fewer die in childhood and fewer hands are needed to work to put food on the table. Developed societies stabilize in size over time. Children move from the workplace into the school, and wages increase as productivity increases.

The common people of advanced societies enjoy luxuries and foods that were not even available to kings of centuries past. The problem for some people is that all of those luxuries and foods are not available to those people in the most backward, poverty-stricken areas. When you realize that voluntary trade is based on mutual gain, and that societies that engage in economic freedom are the ones that develop out of destitution into prosperity, the solution to the problem of poor societies will stare you in the face. What they need is more freedom, incentives for individuals to accumulate personal wealth, stronger protection of their property rights against aggression from individuals and businesses, and less oppression by their own government. The responses of Christians who ignore those extremely important facts will be flailing at the leaves of the tree while the root of the problem grows.

The modern mindset among many people in free societies is apathy toward the gift of freedom that they so richly enjoy. They take for granted the things that they have, and assume it has always been and will always be that way. They appeal to government to do for them what they should do for themselves and for others. It is a very unhealthy situation, both for the developed countries and for those societies that look to them for an example of success. Little by little, they become dependent, much as the Israelites did under Pharaoh. Dependence is slavery.

Jesus gave the template for Christians to make a difference. He actually went out and preached the Good News of the kingdom, he healed people, and he fed the poor. One thing never recorded in the gospels was a call upon a bureaucrat to set up a program and take resources from others to do his work. He rather showed a marked disdain for the bureaucrats of his day. There is a lot of work to be done. All of us aren't healers or preachers or miracle workers. All people can, however, use their own resources to help with the work.

They can establish or work with charitable organizations. Everyone has some level of the traditional three Ts, time, talent, and treasures. They can help and support those on the front lines of Christian missionary work.

Moreover, everyone has a mind to think about consequences. When a program flies in the face of economic law, when government intervenes in prices and quantities on markets or when one group seeks to benefit at the expense of another, speak out against it. Remember that economic laws are not negotiable or compassionate. Good intentions hurt people when they are wielded carelessly. Millennia of recorded history attest to the disasters guaranteed by policies that deny rights and subvert natural or economic law.

Always view political solutions with a skeptical eye. Government planners are not the savior and are not omniscient to make the right decisions for millions of people. Government service does not make someone an angel, and, in fact, presents very strong temptation to use power for one's own selfish purposes. A conflict of interest will usually be resolved in favor of the one with the political power.

In the case of truly abusive rulers, Moses' response would be "Let my people go!" Giving corrupt rulers billions of dollars of foreign aid only entrenches them in their power. It does not help the poor. It does not create development. It is merely the false charity of wealthy development "experts." It is time to face the music and get on with addressing the real problems of corruption, socialism, and tyranny.

Much of this book has been devoted to the idea of freedom and its beneficial economic effects for society. Much of the bible is also devoted to God freeing his people, and the people resisting and turning away from faith. As Moses led his people out of Egypt, the people grumbled and complained. They would rather have gone back into bondage, where at least they were secure in their slavery.

Freedom is difficult. It requires responsibility, discipline, and self-control. It requires faith and reliance on God. It has no assurances and guarantees. It does, however, have its magnificent rewards to those who persevere.

You can make a difference by being faithful, by embracing the freedom with which God has blessed you, and by not using that freedom as a pretext for evil, but rather as a launching pad for faithful witness. The biblical principles embodied in the Commandments are necessarily in alignment with all natural laws, including the laws of economics, because they are part and parcel of God's ordered world.

Concluding Thoughts

The law of the LORD is perfect, reviving the soul. The statutes of the LORD are trustworthy, making wise the simple. (Ps 19:7)

As Christians, we are bound by the Ten Commandments as a guide for action in our lives. We are more so bound to a higher level by Jesus' admonishment to love our neighbor. Love and compassion form a foundation for Christian thought and policy. Too often, however, that compassion is covered with foggy thinking about the way things work in society. A soft heart is accompanied by a soft head. Fairy tale-wishes displace the laws of God's ordered world. Empty rhetoric replaces God's powerful message. Many people look to the government as savior and the source of compassion, and lose sight of the true Savior and the promises he shared with all of us.

Economic laws are neither good nor bad. They are simply descriptions of reality. They are a part of the orderly nature of God's creation, and help to describe that creation, much the same as physical and chemical principles help to describe the physical world.

We briefly examined a number of official policy positions put forth by many churches, government bodies, and organizations and whether they fit with God's law and the laws of economics. While many sound plausible and are based on good intentions, they are destined to failure because they are built on a foundation of economic fallacy.

There are literally hundreds of the same types of programs and it is not practical to discuss each one in detail. A similar investigation can be performed on them, however, and, I hope, you are armed to make your own analysis of them. Most of them involve the "Broken-Window Fallacy," the tendency to look only at what is seen here and now, while ignoring the very real but less obvious effects that are unseen and longer term. They typically involve the use of government force to redistribute something from one person to someone else. In all cases, that type of redistribution is theft on a collective basis rather than on an individual basis. The hubris of central planning is also an important part of the failure of programs aimed at the stated goal of helping the poor and oppressed.

All of the commandments that apply to individuals also apply to governments, since individuals can only delegate those activities that they have a right to do on their own. There is no legitimacy for delegating the use of aggressive force and coercion to governments when those who delegate have no right to use that force and coercion. The commandments give a very good summary of the requirements of God. The law of love, as described by Jesus, lifts them to a higher level and serves as an umbrella statement of what God requires. That law of love, however, in no way negates the requirements of the commandments. It only gives them new perspective. If you love your neighbor, you will not steal, you will not injure, and you will not covet what he or she has. More so, you will recognize that God requires you to do something, to be an active part in the kingdom: ". . . faith by itself, if it is not accompanied by action, is dead." (Jas 2:17)

In modern times, the laws of economics have come to be associated with complex mathematical formulas and macroeconomic models. In spite of the shrouds of mystery surrounding the high priests of economics and the products of their deep thinking, true economic principles are not very difficult to understand. The artificially imposed complexity is a serious impediment to real progress in society and is a justification for domineering arrogance. The high priests of Jesus' time had much the same arrogance in their attitude toward the common Jews because of their inability to read the law.

If you take one thing from reading this book, I hope that it will be an appreciation of the simplicity of true economic principles and their application to real life. They apply to everyday interactions in society because they describe the logic of human interaction. What they don't do is justify huge government programs and macroeconomic tinkering.

It is important that we recognize that Jesus is the Savior. It is right and good that we put our faith in that saving power. It is not right and good that we put our faith in politicians who have a vested interest in abusing their power. No matter how good their intentions seem, they are merely human beings, with all of the weaknesses that every person shares.

History supplies us with many opportunities to see economics at work. It is difficult to connect the dots, however, to relate cause and effect, when the long-lasting effects of decades of bad policies from the past continue to rear their ugly heads. As Christians, we have a role to play in modern economic and political discussions. We must be champions of the truth, champions of the gospel, and champions of the commandments.

Using the tools of correct economic principles, we can look beyond the rhetoric to the substance of a program or policy to see whether the good intentions will bring good results. We can see if it follows the commandments not to steal or covet, or by implication, not to coerce or injure others through the implements of government. We can see if it truly protects citizens from the depredations of others.

God's creation is amazing. The abundance he gave is the raw material for solving all of the problems of our existence here on earth. His natural laws help us find order and a certain amount of predictability. While the future is unknowable and uncertain, we are able to order our own lives and to use our resources, our skills, and our knowledge to make a better life in the future, for ourselves, our families, and for others as we add value through our productivity.

The Christian gospel is one that creates harmony between people. Economics, rightly understood, reflects the laws of God. It is a way to understand human society and how human cooperation works for the good of all. Living according to voluntary trade and respect for the rights of others as outlined in the commandments will guarantee the highest level of cooperation and minimize conflict among all who participate. There truly is a harmony between economics and the Christian gospel.

As we move toward obedience to God, we will no longer be tossed back and forth by the waves and blown here and there by every wind of teaching and by the cunning and craftiness of men in their deceitful scheming. As the Apostle Paul eloquently stated, then we will no longer be infants, but rather mature adults, armed with knowledge and the strength of God's hand.

Acknowledgements

This book began as an informal catalog of my personal efforts to reconcile biblical teachings and the doctrines of the modern churches with what I knew to be true in the economy, in business, and in modern society. Over the years I have bounced ideas off of so many people, read so many books, and wrote and refined those ideas so many times that the contributors to particular sections of this work are innumerable and essentially unidentifiable.

Not everyone agreed with my thoughts, but their sincere arguments challenged me to rethink and refine some more. I thank all of those people who did challenge me. I learned more from trying to find the answers than I did from anything else. Many still probably don't agree with me, but they gave me confidence that I have at least some level of coherence in the discussions that I present.

A number of years ago someone suggested that I write a book, and, though I don't remember who it was, I eventually took him or her up on the idea. Whoever you are, thank you. This has been the most intense, educational journey of my life. It has forced me to research great thinkers in economics, politics, and philosophy, to develop a comprehensive view, and to organize my thoughts in a way that was not possible through other means. It has helped me as a thinker and as a doer.

There are some landmarks in any journey that represent turning points, and one that occurred in this journey was my accidental discovery of the book, *Human Action*, by Ludwig von Mises, a number of years ago. It led me to the Austrian school of economic thought, around which this book revolves. I had finally found the key that brought order and coherence to my thoughts. It resolved my frustration with the incoherence of mainstream economics.

I thank the Ludwig von Mises Institute, the Foundation for Economic Education, The Acton Institute for Religion and Liberty, and other excellent organizations, for their wealth of resources, their insights, and their commitment to free markets and free people. Truth is timeless, and as I was spurred to romp through the centuries of economic thought, it became clear to me that, if economic ideas are indeed true, they had to be just as true in biblical times. As with any book of old, the Bible takes on new meaning when viewed through the lens of timeless economic principles.

The gospel of Jesus is ultimately a call to personal responsibility and freedom. I have come to understand that there is no conflict between true economic principles and the Bible. Those principles are recognizable in the actions of everyone throughout the entire text. They are still with us today to guide us and to help to understand the world around us.

I specifically thank Lawrence Read, president of the Foundation for Economic Education, for writing the forward for this book and for his helpful words of encouragement. He is an inspiration to many people.

I also thank my editor, Dr. James T. McDonough, Jr. for his excellent comments and wonderful insights. He disagreed with me on the substance of many topics, and we had fruitful exchanges that sharpened the edge on my thoughts. He taught me a lot about the art of writing and had a significant influence on the final article. I do, however, take full responsibility for the end result and any errors that may have slipped in after his skillful editing work.

Finally, I give my undying love and appreciation to my wonderful wife and children for their loving support over the years. Thank you.

Appendix 1

The Irrelevance of Macroeconomics

The fundamental concepts discussed in this book are typically thought of as microeconomics. The mainstream assumption is that microeconomics helps to understand economics at the micro, or local, level—the firm, the individual. In order to understand the macro economy, on the national or international scale, more sophisticated methods, using aggregate statistics and complex mathematical models, are deemed necessary.

Inherent in the model building is the presumption that models should be used for policy prescriptions for politicians. Model builders and users assume that, if only they can model the real economy closely enough and predict the future accurately enough, then political programs can be designed to maximize real economic outcomes, presumably for the benefit of the citizens. There are many problems with this line of thinking:

1. Known cause effect relationships are disregarded.
2. Historical artifacts can't be used to predict the future.
3. The circumstances of individual decision makers often change.
4. Each local area is a different economy.
5. Complex economies have too many variables.
6. Planners make mistakes and often are corrupted by power.
7. God-given rights trump central planning.

The opinion of this author, and that of many economics

professors and professionals,[41] is that the presumed division between micro and macro economics is arbitrary and artificial. There is only one economics, and the economic laws always apply.

All economic activity is the result of choices made by individuals, based on their circumstances and assumptions about how the world works. The macro economy is merely a composite of the actions of individual decision makers, whether they are in individual households, international corporations or high-level government offices. The phenomena in a society emerge from the interactions and, as a complex adaptive system, the emergent effects change in response to the billions of inputs that constantly occur.

Expanded discussion of weaknesses inherent in macroeconomics:

1. Known cause/effect relationships are disregarded.

---

[41] Many economists, particularly those of the Austrian School, hold the view that mainstream macroeconomics, as currently practiced, is an abuse of mathematics and statistics, and rests on profoundly mistaken assumptions.

The Austrian School of economics is a well-established school of thought. It has nothing to do with Austria, but rather it emerged in Vienna as an intellectual movement a century and a half ago. Its proponents now live all over the world, a large portion of them in America. Austrian economics starts from the assumption that all economic phenomena arise from individual human actors making decisions.

It builds on a coherent logic of human action to understand economic events as they occur in the real world, but the emphasis on individual responsibility and freedom and respect for the life and property of others reinforces and supports the commandments and the gospel of Jesus.

See the list of references for further reading on Austrian Economics.

The validity of the laws of economics, such as supply and demand, is accepted by nearly all economists, including mainstream macroeconomists. Once the jump is made to the macro sphere, however, the link between prices, supply, and demand is assumed to be severed, and statistical correlations are substituted for the logic of human action. Artificial relationships are developed that affect significant public policy. Employment policy is seen by many macroeconomists as a choice between more inflation or more unemployment.

Persistent unemployment, however, is simply a glut in the supply of labor in a particular local market, due to the price of labor in that market being held artificially above its market price. Acute unemployment typically is related to government interventions that make businesses uncompetitive and drive them away or into bankruptcy. On the other hand, independent of unemployment, inflation in the popular sense, meaning the general rise in prices, is caused by inflation in the technical sense, the increase in the supply of money by monetary authorities and fractional-reserve banks. The correlation between the two occurs only because economic tinkering by politicians affects all aspects of the economy. The linking of the two by macroeconomic modelers is an instance of the abuse of statistics to justify further intervention in the economy.

The laws of economics are supported by consistent logic, confirmed by historical fact. Macroeconomic models are supported by statistical analysis of data, with little support from underlying logic. Friedrich August von Hayek (1899–1992), a Nobel laureate in economics, addressed this issue in his Nobel Prize acceptance speech, entitled, "The Pretense of Knowledge."

". . . often that is treated as important which happens to be accessible to measurement. This is sometimes carried to the point where it is demanded that our theories must be formulated in such terms that they refer only to measurable magnitudes. It can hardly be denied that such a demand quite arbitrarily limits the facts which are to be admitted as possible causes of the events which occur in the real world."

He further states: "But the effects on policy of the more ambitious constructions have not been very fortunate and I confess that I prefer true but imperfect knowledge, even if it leaves much indetermined and unpredictable, to a pretense of exact knowledge that is likely to be false."

We are living, at this moment, with the very unfortunate effects on policy of very ambitious constructions that have wrought massive distortion and misery on our society. His words from 1974 ring true today, speaking of economists: "We have indeed at the moment little cause for pride: as a profession we have made a mess of things."

2.Historical artifacts can't be used to predict the future.

While nature and society are subject to a certain order, and we can discern laws that govern phenomena, the future must always, necessarily, be uncertain, unknowable, and unpredictable. It is not plausible to conceive of circumstances of human existence where everything about the future is known in advance. That very knowledge would cause people to use that knowledge to attempt to change future events in their favor.

Weather forecasters rely on complex models of weather systems and have armies of scientists to develop, adjust, and maintain them. Yet, even the best models cannot predict the weather with any degree of accuracy any further out than a day or two. Long-term weather forecasts are notoriously wrong because so many physical events of the future are unknowable.

Weather forecasting uses the simple and known laws of nature to understand patterns as they develop. The farther out the patterns are projected, the more uncertainty enters the picture, and the more that disturbing, disruptive influences throw off the expected results.

The same effect necessarily prevails with macroeconomic models. While there are simple laws of economics, the patterns we see in an economy are the result of prior inputs of millions or billions of people and changing environmental factors. Statistics based on those measured effects are merely historical artifacts.

There is no reason to believe that these same inputs will exist tomorrow, next year, or next decade. It is impossible to know and, even more so, to take into account the incredible number of variables that affect an economy every day. Given that economic systems are as chaotic and as constantly changing as weather systems, it is implausible that an economic model can be any more reliable than a weather model; that is, the best projections would be obsolete after a few of days. That is obviously the case in reality.

The pretense of knowledge was on public display during the economic boom leading to the housing bubble and the economic woes starting in 2008. The economic models gave no warning of the dire economic situation, but rather suggested continuing growth. It may be argued that it is unreasonable to expect perfect predictions from economic models, since weather forecasters often make errors in their predictions.

The disturbing fact is that, not only did the economic modelers fail to predict the most significant economic hurricane bearing down on us since the 1930s, they vehemently denied its existence until the moment it struck in full force. That isn't forgivable, given the condescending arrogance with which the models are sold to the public. It is, however, understandable. It is impossible for mathematical models to predict the future.

3. The circumstances of decision makers change often.

The aggregate measures used in models are compilations of large numbers of transactions of many people over a wide area. The statistics ignore the individuals as decision makers, with vast differences in preferences, goals, and assumptions about the future, which constantly change. Weather models are descriptions of complex mechanical systems made up of elements with definite, unchanging properties. In contrast, economic systems are made up of human beings, whose primary characteristic is that they make choices and change their minds. People react to events, but they also react to predictions, perceptions, measurement, and even attempts to control and manipulate them.

Fads and fashions change on a regular basis, and people have a tendency to be fickle. Families don't always go on the same vacations. Businesses adopt new technologies, build new factories, or go bankrupt. Wars break out, and politicians pass new laws. Society is in a constant state of change that is significant but unpredictable.

The models fail to predict economic meltdowns because, no matter how good the statistics are and how large the numbers, the modelers insert their own biases into the models out of necessity. With only historical artifacts to go by, the model of the future will reflect what the modeler expects. Reality, however, doesn't follow their rules.

4.Each local area is a different economy.

Aggregate measures covering wide geographic and demographic areas ignore the immense variety of local conditions, geography, climate, and periodic phenomena. Macroeconomics and statistical aggregates can describe what happened in an economy, much the same as the National Football League can produce statistics on total scores, yards of offense, and so forth. Those statistics, however, can never be used to truly understand the game of football, nor can they adequately control the play. A team wins because each player takes certain actions based on the situation on the field at the time. That situation changes from minute to minute, game to game, and season to season. Each interested party, the owners, coaches, players, fans, hot-dog venders, and so on, all do what they do because they expect it to give the best result, given their own goals, assumptions, and circumstances.

Models based on aggregate statistics of a football league cannot take into account such things as individual player motivation, crowd support, weather at game time, field conditions, and so forth. There is no aggregate playing surface. Some fields have grass, some have artificial turf. There is no aggregate crowd. Some stadiums are always sold out, others have trouble filling the seats. There are no aggregate coaches. Each one has his own strengths and weaknesses. There are no aggregate players. They are different ages, levels of experience, physical strength, and mental maturity.

The American national economy includes the Appalachian Region, a poor rural area. It also includes the Hamptons, with the homes of millionaires and billionaires. It includes dense metropolitan areas, rural farmland, and barren desert. Each of these areas has a different economy, different advantages, different challenges. There is no macroeconomic solution that can possibly meet the needs of every area of the country, nor the 300 million people that comprise it. It cannot be a "one size fits all" solution.

Monetary policy determines the value of money for the whole country, and it hinges to a large extent on aggregate employment statistics and economic growth in the national economy. Average unemployment statistics mean, however, that some areas are higher than the average and some are lower. That being the case, a generic national policy is, at best, a solution to problems that don't exist for many areas, causing distortion of the local economies. It is the solution to the wrong problem.

The application of national fiscal policy can only take place by taking money and resources involuntarily from one person or group and giving it to others. Economic stimulation of the group that gets the resources comes at the expense of economic de-stimulation of the group whose resources are taken. Some individuals, businesses, and localities benefit greatly from fiscal spending. It hurts others, however, because the money comes from their pockets.

5.Complex economies have too many variables.

A national economy has millions of people with changing tastes and preferences, different geographic regions with changing weather patterns, changing seasons, unexpected natural disasters, and so on. Even if all of the variables were able to be exactly measurable, the models built on them would include so many variables that the models would be hopelessly complex. It makes modeling of the whole a useless exercise at best. Without taking all of the significant variables of the present and the unknown future into account, however, the very precise results attained by the models are nothing more than the pretense of knowledge so eloquently described by F. A. Hayek.[42]

He is right to believe that it is better to have an understanding that is true, even though we may not know all of the underlying details, than it is to have a very exact knowledge that is likely to be false.

6.Planners make mistakes and are corrupted by power.

Nobody is perfect. Everybody makes mistakes. When an individual makes a mistake, it usually affects him or her and a limited number of other people. When a business person makes a mistake, more people are affected. Employees may lose their jobs, suppliers may lose sales, and so forth. The bigger the entity that is subject to the mistake, the more people will be affected negatively.

---

[42] *The Pretense Of Knowledge* is the late F. A. Hayek's Nobel Prize lecture delivered in 1974.

The same holds true for politicians and bureaucrats. The higher the level of government at which the mistakes are made, the more people that are hurt.

Central planning necessarily entails high-level government officials making decisions that affect millions of people. The plans, being based on unreliable economic models, are necessarily prone to large mistakes. Those mistakes have had disastrous consequences in every nation where central planning holds sway. The latest economic meltdown in America and the world is simply the current installment of induced disaster.

A related and likely more important issue is Lord Acton's famous dictum that "Power corrupts, and absolute power corrupts absolutely." Central planning necessarily involves the concentration of government power in the hands of those at the top, those who can use the coercive power of government to enforce their will. Economic models can be designed to support whatever ideology the central planner wants to impose. While the models have little relation to the real laws of economics, they don't need to. All they need is the appeal to power and enforcement, something that politicians and dictators are all too willing to accommodate.

7.God-Given rights trump central planning.

The rights of individuals arise from the requirements of the commandments. Stealing, injury, aggression, and covetousness are prohibited. That being the case, no one has the right to delegate theft, injury, aggression, or covetousness to anyone else, including those individuals designated as government officials.

Where oppression exists, it is, in all cases, either directly inflicted by government officials or indirectly aided and abetted by them. When Jesus spoke of freeing the oppressed, he was talking of people under the thumb of either those in government or those with powerful government connections, who could oppress with little threat of reprisal.

Macroeconomic policy ignores the God-given rights of people to make their own decisions about their lives and their property. It assumes that it is right and proper for government to take from one person to give to another and to interfere in the lives of the citizens.

The gospel of Jesus is the gospel of freedom as well as the gospel of love. We are called to help others while we take responsibility for our own lives. We can delegate neither our love nor our personal responsibility to government.

Appendix 2

Recommended Reading

Resources, Web Sites and Publications:

The Acton Institute for the Study of Religion and Liberty
http://www.acton.org/

The Ludwig Von Mises Institute
www.mises.org

The Foundation for Economic Education
www.fee.org

Institute of Economic Affairs
www.iea.org

The Cato Institute
www.cato.org

The Library of Economics and Liberty
econlib.org

Recommended Books:

The Conquest of Poverty, Henry Hazlitt

Essentials of Economics, Faustino Ballvé

Common Sense Economics, James Gwartney, Richard Stroup, and Dwight R. Lee.

Not A Zero-Sum Game, Manuel F. Ayau

Economics on Trial Mark Skousen, Ph.D.

Economics in One Lesson, Henry Hazlitt

The Failure of the New Economics, Henry Hazlitt

Human Action, Ludwig Von Mises

The Anticapitalist Mentality, Ludwig Von Mises

Man, Economy, and State, Murray N. Rothbard

The Mystery of Capital, Hernando De Soto

The Noblest Triumph, Tom Bethel

The Economic Way of Thinking, Paul Heyne, Peter Boettke and David Prychitko

How the West Grew Rich, Nathan Rosenburg and L. E. Birdzell

Forty Centuries of Price Controls, Robert Schuettinger and Eamonn Butler

How Capitalism Saved America, Thomas J. DiLorenzo

It's Getting Better All the Time, Stephen Moore and Julian

Simon

The Resourceful Earth, Julian Simon and Herman Kahn

The Ultimate Resource, Julian Simon

Misesian Economics and the Bible, Essay by Mark W. Hendrickson

Free to Choose, Milton and Rose Friedman

Against the Tide, Douglas A. Irwin

Prosperity Versus Planning, David Osterfeld

Crisis and Leviathan, Robert Higgs

The Tariff Idea, W. M. Curtiss

Out of Work, Richard Veddar and Lowell Gallaway

America's Great Depression, Murray N. Rothbard

The Great Depression, Lionel Robbins

Poverty Cure, a video series by The Acton Institute

APPENDIX 3
SCRIPTURE INDEX

aggregate statistics, 7, 67
   macroeconomics, 194-203
Agricultural Adjustment Act, 15
agriculture, 42, 58, 162
Amish, 99
ancient civilizations, xvi, 65, 145
antitrust, 85
Aramean army, 40
arbitrary government, 64-65, 178
Armentano, Dominick T., 85
assumptions
   about the future, 4, 16, 146, 199
   about good and bad, 5, 90
   decisions based on, 20, 142, 195
   determinant of value, 146
Austrian economics, 192
banking, 67, 180, 183
bankruptcy, 165, 196
banks, 50, 151, 179-183, 196
Bastiat, Frédéric, 78
Bauer, Peter T., xxviii, 171, 173
benefit
   cost and, 6, 25
   value of time, 17
Bethel, Tom, 101
black market, 15, 82, 133
broken-window fallacy, 78-79, 189
   politics, xx, 99
bureaucracy, 64-65, 78, 104, 143, 173
Burkhauser, Richard V., 126, 129
business cycle, 67
Butler, Eamonn, 78
buy local/buy American, 145-148

capital
   accumulation, xii, 60,65, 68, 139, 149
   and productivity, 59, 97, 103, 139
   investment, 54, 59, 64, 103
   flywheel of progress, 62-64, 68
   property rights, 101-105
   trade and, 64-66
cartels, 84
cause-effect relationships, 194
central banks, 179-183
central planning, 159, 176, 189, 194
   concentration of power, 202
   development economics, xxvii, 171-174
   health care markets, 159, 160, 164
   opposed to rights, 202
   political elite, 160
centurion, 123
charity
   development economics, xxvii, 173
   false, 164, 186
   good Samaritan model, 121, 161
   insurance premiums, 161, 168, 169
   importance of, xxvii, 16, 122, 143
   wealth and, 96, 157
choice, xii,16, 97
   and freedom, xxvi, 8
   costs and benefits, 6, 146
   economic thinking, xvii, 145, 195
   limited resources, 42, 71
   relevant quantities, 21
   restrictions on, 9, 81, 160

ABOUT THE AUTHOR
DANIEL J. MCLAUGHLIN

Daniel J. McLaughlin was Certified Public Accountant and a corporate finance officer for most of his career, but now focuses his efforts as a writer, consultant, and entrepreneur. He holds a bachelor of science degree from Cornell University and a bachelor of science in accounting degree, Summa Cum Laude, from the State University of New York at Fredonia.

Mr. McLaughlin is co-founder of several NGOs in Africa and advisor to and investor in several startup enterprises there, believing that entrepreneurship and the ideas of freedom and markets are the solutions to the problems of poverty and lack of development.

His writing focuses on economic and political issues, with a weekly column published since 2006. Visit his website where his columns, other writings, and related activities can be found.

daniel-mclaughlin.com

Other related websites:

compassionandtruth.com

aboutfreedom.org